P-61 BLACK WIDOW in action

By Larry Davis And Dave Menard
Color By Don Greer
And Perry Manley
Illustrated by Joe Sewell

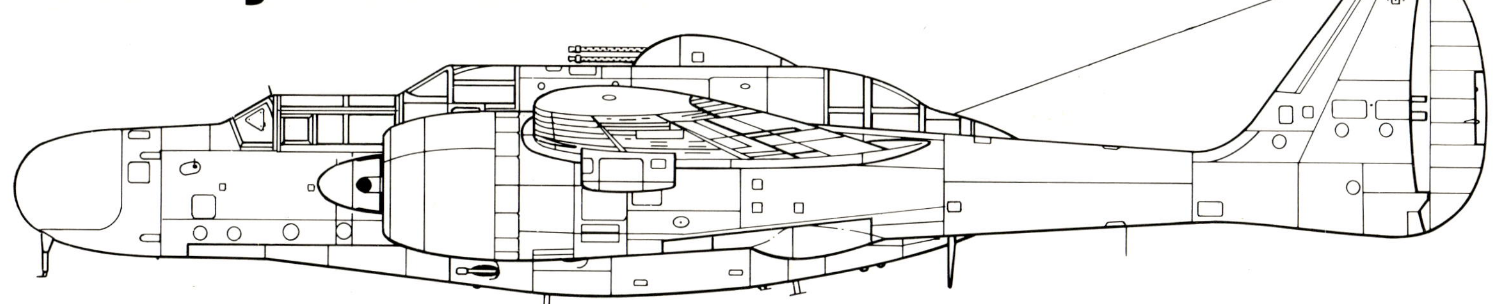

Aircraft Number 106
squadron/signal publications

LT Herman Ernst shot down a German V-1 Buzz Bomb over the English Channel on 15 July 1944 while flying *BORROWED TIME*, a P-61A of the 422nd Night Fighter Squadron.

ISBN 0-89747-248-9

If you have any photographs of the aircraft, armor, soldiers or ships of any nation, particularly wartime snapshots, why not share them with us and help make Squadron/Signal's books all the more interesting and complete in the future. Any photograph sent to us will be copied and the original returned. The donor will be fully credited for any photos used. Please send them to:

Squadron/Signal Publications, Inc.
1115 Crowley Drive.
Carrollton, TX 75011-5010.

Dedication

This book is dedicated to the memory of John K. 'Jack' Northrop —whose farsighted designs are only now being fully appreciated.

Acknowledgements

Air Force Museum
Robert Bolinder
Jeff Ethell
George Kerstetter
David McLaren
Mid Atlantic Air Museum
Merle Olmsted
Carroll Smith
Jim Sullivan
Dick Wood
James Crow
Gene Yagan
Alvin Andersen
Dr. Ira Chart
Arthur Harrison
Ernie McDowell
David Menard
Northrop Aviation
John Raths
Russell Strine
Ernest Thomas
Peter Bowers
Robert Hernandez
David H. Klaus

When an RAF officer first saw the P-61, he exclaimed, *"My God, look at the size of the bloody beast! Only the Americans could dream that one up!"* This pair of P-61s parked on a French airfield during 1944 were assigned to the 425th NFS. (AFM)

Introduction

The Northrop P-61 Black Widow was the only American aircraft designed as a night-fighter to be produced during the Second World War. The Black Widow proved to be a deadly night-fighter in combat against both the Germans and Japanese.

The P-61 was designed by John (Jack) Knudson Northrop, who was one of the most farsighted aviation engineers of all time. His aircraft were innovative and usually ahead of their time. This is highlighted by the fact that the Northrop B-2 Stealth Bomber can trace its development back to the Northrop Flying Wings of the 1930s and 1940s.

Northrop Aircraft Inc. was formed during August of 1939 with Jack Northrop as President and Chief Engineer. Within a year, Northrop had moved his company into a new 122,000 square foot plant at Hawthorne, California, and was employing over 100 people. At first, Northrop did subcontract work for other manufacturers — tail sections for PBY Catalinas and engine nacelles for B-17s. Additionally, Northrop built the Vultee Vengeance dive bomber under license for the Royal Air Force. It was this program that led to Northrop's most successful aircraft for the Second World War.

Northrop was in London meeting with the British on Vengeance production plans during the German night raids of 1940 (known as the Blitz). At the time, the RAF had nothing that could stop the Luftwaffe night raids (neither did any other country). Day-fighters, such as Spitfires and Hurricanes, were scrambled, but by the time they located their targets, the bombers had already dropped their bombs. The British wanted a night interceptor and outlined their needs to all the aircraft manufacturers they were dealing with, including Jack Northrop.

The British requirement called for an aircraft capable of staying airborne all night (at least eight hours) and with the speed necessary to catch night raiders before they dropped their bombs. Northrop realized that to meet the fuel requirement and be able to carry the specified armament of multiple gun turrets, the aircraft had to be big and twin engined.

During this same time, the Army Air Corps also expressed an interest in a purpose built night-fighter. LT GEN Delos Emmons, Commander, Headquarters, Army Air Corps, had also been in London during the Blitz. When he returned to the U.S. during the Summer of 1940, Emmons began pressing his case for an American night-fighter. During the Fall of 1940, the Emmons Board issued a preliminary specification for a night-fighter design and on 21 October 1940, COL Lawrence Craigie of the Air Technical Service Command called Vladimir Pavlecka (Northrop's Chief of Research) to Wright Field. COL Craigie explained the Army's needs and told Pavlecka not to take any notes, "Just try and keep this in your memory!"

The requirement called for a twin-engined aircraft designed to fly and fight at night. The mission was, "The interception and destruction of hostile aircraft in flight during periods of darkness or under conditions of poor visibility." The aircraft was to be manned by a pilot and one other crew member and, while COL Craigie outlined the armament requirements, there was absolutely no mention of radar (other than a vague reference that the aircraft would carry a "device which would locate enemy aircraft in the dark").

The following morning Pavlecka met with Jack Northrop to discuss the requirement. Northrop compared the Air Corps specifications with those issued by the RAF (which Northrop had been working on for over a month) and within a week Northrop was ready to answer the Army. On 5 November 1940, Northrop and Pavlecka met with Air Material Command officers at Wright Field to present their proposal. They had one competitor, the Douglas XA-26A night-fighter proposal. In any event, the Northrop proposal was selected.

Northrop's initial night-interceptor design called for an aircraft with a long fuselage pod slung between two engine nacelles/booms. Each nacelle would house a Pratt & Whitney R-2800 Double Wasp eighteen cylinder, air-cooled, radial engine. The nacelles tapered back into booms with a vertical stabilizer and rudder assembly. The two booms would be connected by a large, single horizontal stabilizer and elevator. The fuselage would house a crew of three, the radar unit, and two four-gun turrets. The turrets were mounted in the nose and tail and were armed with four .50 caliber Browning machine guns. The design was huge for a fighter, having a length of forty-five feet six inches, a wingspan of sixty-six feet and a projected weight of 22,600 pounds when fully loaded and armed.

The aircraft was designed to use tricycle landing gear and the wings housed the Northrop-designed "Zap flaps" — a full-span retractable flap. Several changes were investigated before the design was finalized, including the use of a single vertical stabilizer/rudder design. One change that was accepted was the replacement of the nose and tail turrets with upper and lower fuselage turrets incorporating a second gunner.

During late November of 1940, the design reverted to the original three man/twin rudder/vertical stabilizer configuration. The Air Corps, however, wanted more firepower and directed that the lower fuselage gun turret be replaced by four wing mounted 20MM cannons. This proposal, Northrop Specification 8A, was formally submitted to the Army Air Material Command at Wright Field on 5 December 1940. With some minor changes, the Northrop NS-8A proposal met all the Army's requirements and a Letter of Authority For Purchase was issued to Northrop on 17 December 1940 with a formal contract calling for two experimental aircraft and two small scale models of the proposed aircraft (at a cost not to exceed $1,367,000.00) awarded on 10 January 1941. The contract assigned the NS-8A the military designation XP-61.

With the award of the experimental contract, Northrop immediately began work on the first prototype. The prototype contract was quickly followed (on 10 March 1941) with a second contract calling for thirteen YP-61 service test aircraft. During that same month, the Army/Navy Standardization Committee decided to standardize both ser-

The first XP-61 (41-19509) was officially rolled out on 8 May 1942. The aircraft was overall Natural Metal with Yellow engine cowlings, the finish normally applied to Northrop factory test aircraft. The stripes on the main landing gear tires were for photographic use during taxi tests. (AFM)

vices on the use of updraft carburetors for all aircraft engines. The XP-61 had been designed to use downdraft carburetors and Northrop estimated it would take at least two months to redesign the engine nacelle to accommodate the change. Luckily, the committee changed its decision and no time was lost.

The XP-61 prototype was powered by two 2,000 hp Pratt & Whitney R-2800-25S air cooled, radial engines equipped with two stage, two speed mechanical superchargers. It was felt that turbo-superchargers were not needed for the XP-61's proposed mission, even though the addition of a turbo-supercharger would have added approximately 50 mph in top speed and 10,000 feet to the aircraft's ceiling.

On 2 April 1941 the Air Corps Mockup Board met at Northrop to review the XP-61 mockup. As a result of their review, several changes were made to the aircraft. The wing guns were relocated to the underside of the fuselage, flame arrestors were added to the engine exhausts and some of the radio gear was redistributed. With the removal of the guns and ammunition from the wing, the capacity of the wing fuel tanks was increased from 540 to 646 gallons. Additionally, the board required that provisions be made for the use of external fuel tanks. These changes, especially the redesign of the lower fuselage to house the cannons, added over thirty days to an already delayed schedule.

The heart of the XP-61 would be its Airborne Interception (AI) Radar system. The AI radar evolved from a modified SCR-268 Searchlight Controller Radar, which had been flight tested in a modified Douglas B-18A. By 18 June 1941, the National Defense Research Committee's Radiation Laboratory had completed its initial development work on the AI radar which was slated for installation in the XP-61. This radar, designated the SCR-720, was produced by Western Electric Company.

Production SCR-720A radars had a scanning radio transmitter mounted in the nose of the aircraft with a range of almost five miles in AI mode. The SCR-720A could also be used as an airborne beacon or homing service, a navigational aid, and for operations in conjunction with interrogator-responder (Identification Friend or Foe-IFF) equipment. The radar operator in the XP-61 would locate and track the target and once within range, the pilot would close for the kill using a scope mounted in the center of his instrument panel. The upper turret on the XP-61 could be controlled and fired by any member of the three man crew. The Radar Operator (RO) could traverse the turret 180 degrees to fire on targets approaching from the rear or elevate the guns 90 degrees to engage targets above the XP-61. The forward firing cannon, however, could only be fired by the pilot.

Construction of the two XP-61 prototypes continued through the Summer of 1941, although not without problems. The dorsal turret mounting ring was almost impossible to mount in the aircraft so Northrop opted to use a pedestal mount like that used on the upper turret of a B-17. Then, the turret itself became unavailable from the sub-contractor. Experimental aircraft came second in priority to operational aircraft and the same turret was used in the B-29. As a result, a dummy turret was installed for flight testing. During February of 1942, Curtiss notified Northrop that the C5425-A10 automatic, full-feathering propeller slated for the XP-61, would not be available in time for either the prototype's rollout or early flight tests. As a result, Hamilton Standard propellers were used until the Curtiss units became available. Finally, on 8 May 1942, the first XP-61 prototype (41-19509) rolled off the Hawthorne assembly line.

During the construction of the prototype, the XP-61's weight had increased. The prototype had an empty weight of 22,392 pounds and a takeoff weight of 29,673 pounds. The prototype was powered by two 2,000 hp Pratt & Whitney R-2800-25S Double Wasp radial engines driving Curtiss Electric C5425-A10 12 foot 2 inch diameter four blade propellers. In addition to the Western Electric SCR-720A radar set, the XP-61 carried two command radio sets (SCR-522As) and three other radios (SCR-695A, AN/APG-1 and AN/APG-2). The central fire control system for the gun turret was the General Electric GE2CFR12A3, similar to that used on the B-29.

Taxi tests began almost immediately, and it was during the high speed taxi test on 21 May 1942 that the XP-61 lifted off the runway for the first time. Northrop test pilot Vance Breese officially conducted the XP-61's first flight five days later, on 26 May. Following an uneventful fifteen minute flight, Breese told Jack Northrop that *"...you've got a damn fine airplane!"*

Flight tests revealed that the XP-61 had a stall speed of 75 mph (power on) and 80 mph (power off), a maximum speed of 380 mph, the takeoff roll was slightly over 1,500 feet, rate of climb was 2,000 feet/minute, and range was approximately 1,200 miles. The test pilots reported that the aircraft had to be deliberately put into a spin and it recovered easily by simply relaxing the controls.

As enthusiastic as the flight tests were, the problems with as complex a design as the XP-61 began to overwhelm the program. The XP-61 had been designed and built to incorporate the "Zap" flap: a full-span, retractable flap. Additionally, the aircraft did not use conventional ailerons of any type. Problems were soon encountered with too critical production-line tolerances and the test pilot began reporting unfavorable flying characteristics associated with the "Zap" flap. As a result, these were replaced with four (two inboard and two outboard) conventional flaps and small ailerons. To augment lateral control, Northrop developed the "Northrop Retractable Ailerons," or wing spoilers. The spoilers were large vented panels that acted in conjunction with the ailerons, moving into the air from the upper wing surface and increasing the aircraft's roll rate.

On 1 September 1941, the Army ordered the P-61 into production with an order for some 150 aircraft under the designation P-61 Black Widow. This was before the first XP-61 was completed and reflected the pressing need for night-fighters in all theaters of operations.

The first XP-61 prototype made its maiden flight on 26 May 1942. Shortly after the first flight, the aircraft was painted in overall Flat Black with Red serial numbers, the standard camouflage scheme for American night-fighters. (AFM)

Development

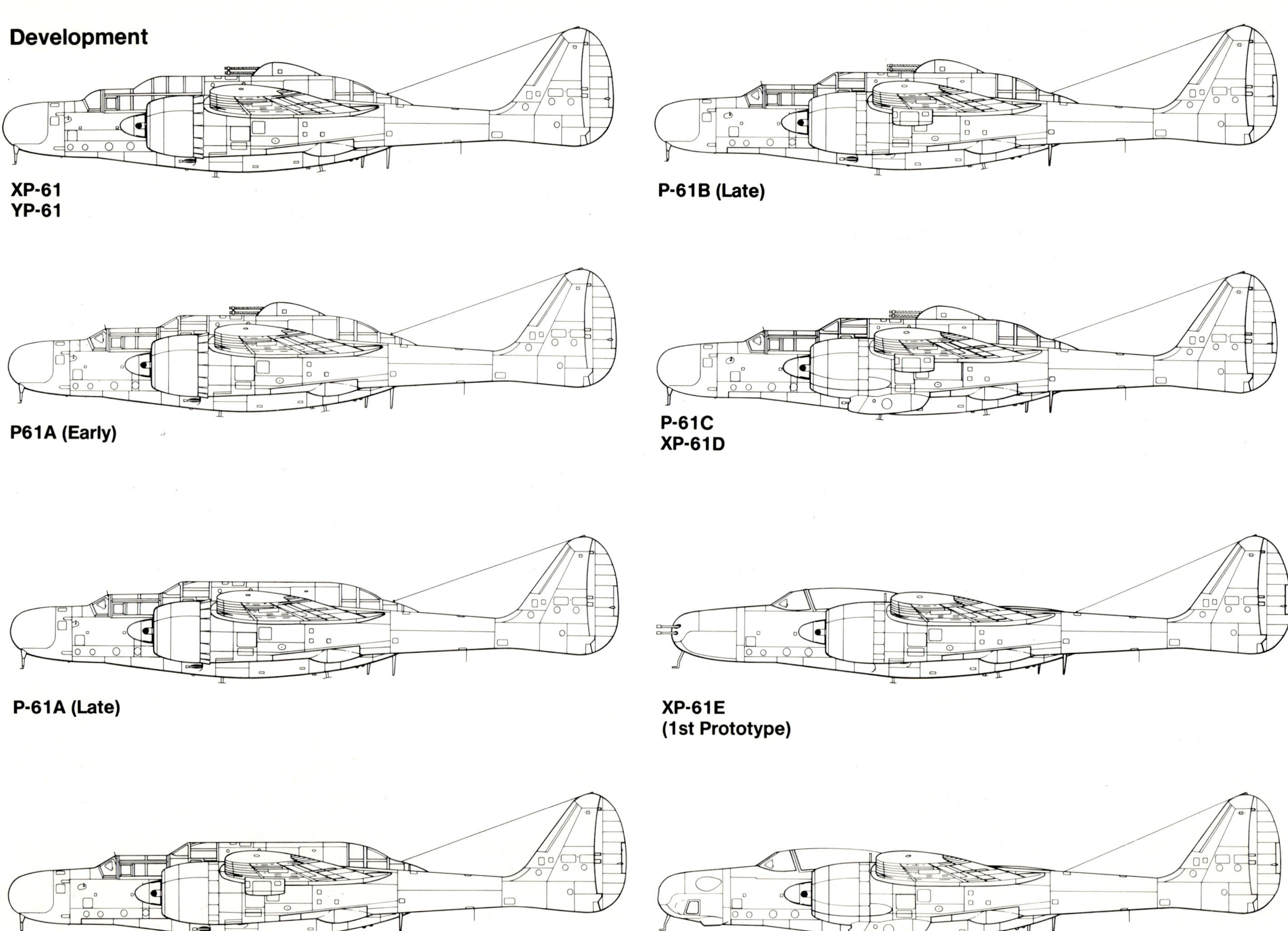

YP-61

Most of the changes ordered by the Army from the tests of the XP-61 were incorporated in the thirteen service test YP-61s, which began coming off the assembly line during early Summer of 1943. Externally, they differed little from the two XP-61 prototypes. The major difference was a change in engines, with the P&W R-2800-25s being replaced by R-2800-10s. The YP-61s were delivered in a Flat Black night-fighter paint scheme (the XP-61s had been delivered in Natural Metal with Yellow cowlings). The Army took delivery of the first YP-61 on 6 August 1943, with the last aircraft (plus a spare static test airframe minus engines) being delivered by September of 1943 at a cost of $649,584.00 per aircraft.

On 12 February 1942 the Army ordered an additional 410 P-61s and followed this with additional orders for some 1,200 P-61s to be built by Northrop at Hawthorne, California, and a second plant which was to be built in Denver, Colorado. These orders included fifty P-61s intended for the RAF under Lend Lease. Later, during July of 1942, these production orders were down-graded to 207 aircraft.

Flight tests with the YP-61s revealed a problem with the dorsal turret which caused severe tail buffeting whenever the turret was moved (elevated or rotated). So severe was the problem, that consideration was given to completely delete the turret from production P-61s. Several quick-fix solutions were tried including adding small airfoils over the guns, deletion of two of the guns, and reinforcing the turret. The easiest solution was to simply fix (lock) the turret to fire forward. The problem ironed itself out during the P-61A program when the turret became unavailable and the aircraft were built without them.

The YP-61s went into service during October of 1943, being issued to the 422nd Night-Fighter Squadron, at Orlando Air Base, Florida. The aircraft served as trainers and no YP-61 ever saw combat. The two XP-61s were relegated to trainer duties at Hawthorne to train mechanics on the P-61.

This YP-61 of the 481st NFOTG at Orlando, carried the name *Black Maria* on the fuselage side in White. The modified two gun dorsal turret was an attempt to alleviate the tail buffet problem. This YP-61 also had an opaque Plexiglas radome. (Jeff Ethell)

One of the thirteen YP-61 service test aircraft in flight over Florida. These aircraft were used as trainers by the 481st Night-Fighter Operational Training Group. The YP-61s had the Zap Flaps of the XP-61s deleted and Northrop Retractable Ailerons (wing spoilers) installed. (AFM)

This YP-61 (41-18888) on the ramp at Orlando has the two gun turret rotated ninety degrees and the guns elevated. The upper turret was intended to defend against rear targets. In operational service, however, the turret was usually locked forward and fired by the pilot. (Northrop)

There were thirteen YP-61 service test aircraft built and most were based at Orlando, Florida with the 481st NFOTG. The 481st was responsible for both flight testing the YP-61 and training flight crews that would fly the P-61 in combat. (McDowell)

This YP-61 (41-18877) of the 481st NFOTG is about to take off on a night test mission during which the P-61's exhaust pattern would be photographed. These photos would be used to train crews on how to identify the P-61 at night by its exhaust pattern. (AFM)

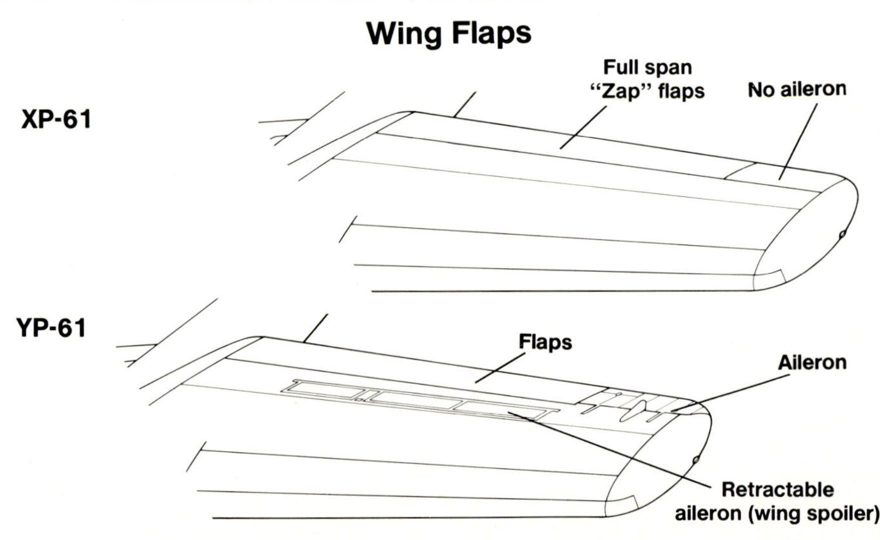

P-61A

Externally, the production P-61A was quite similar to the XP-61 prototypes and YP-61 service test aircraft, differing in the shape of the windscreen/canopy and in the camouflage scheme in which it was delivered. The sloped windscreens on the pilot's and gunner's canopies used on the XP-61 and YP-61 were replaced by sharply angled windscreens that featured armored glass panels.

With tests still going on as to what color was best for night-fighters, the first P-61As off the Hawthorne assembly line were delivered in the standard Army Air Corps camouflage of Olive Drab uppersurfaces over Neutral Gray undersurfaces. Internally, the P-61A had the welded magnesium alloy tail booms of the XP/YP-61 replaced by booms made of aluminum. The first production P-61A rolled off the Hawthorne assembly line during October of 1943, fitted with the four gun dorsal turret.

With the serious tail buffet problem still unsolved and with a pressing requirement for the turrets for the B-29 program making them increasingly difficult to obtain, Northrop decided to delete the dorsal turret from production P-61As beginning with the thirty-eighth aircraft. Although the turret was not fitted, the aircraft were completed with all necessary wiring installed so that the turrets could be retrofitted if they became available later.

Removal of the turret, gunner's seat, and gun sighting equipment saved over 1,600 pounds, giving the P-61A an additional three mph in speed over the YP-61. Minor changes took place throughout P-61A production. Beginning with the 46th production aircraft, the 2,000 hp R-2800-10 engines were replaced with 2,250 hp R-2800-65 engines and aircraft with the new engines were designated P-61A-5s. The P-61A-10 featured engine water-injection to boost power for short periods in combat. The P-61A-11 was the first Black Widow to have provision for underwing pylons (capable of carrying 165 gallon fuel tanks or 1,000 pound bombs).

On 20 July 1943, the Army activated the 481st Night-Fighter Operational Training Group at Orlando Field, Florida. Not only was the 481st responsible for training night-fighter crews for operational units, it also conducted the service tests of the YP-61 and was responsible for night air defense of Florida and the southeastern U.S. Initially, the group had one squadron assigned — the 348th NFS. As the training program developed, squadrons would form as part of the 481st, train their crews, then be issued new aircraft and rotated overseas on their respective combat assignments.

Only two USAAF night-fighter squadrons did not have their crews trained at Orlando. The 6th NFS and 414th NFS were operational night-fighter units equipped with either P-70s or Beaufighters and their P-61As were ferried to them in the combat zone. Initial pilot training for new units was carried out in the Douglas P-70. They trained in ground gunnery, both day and night air gunnery, skip bombing, and night interception tactics. Radar operators received their first training in Beech AT-11s, followed by the YP-61s. The training course was four months long. During January of 1944, the 481st NFOTG moved from Orlando Field to Hammer Field, California.

During March of 1944, the twelfth production P-61A-1 (42-5496) was disassembled, crated, and shipped to England for testing by the RAF. The RAF found that the P-61A lacked speed when compared with the Mosquito night-fighter and after completing their evaluation, they returned the P-61 to the Army Air Force during February of 1945.

Before the P-61s had become available, the Army had tried several different aircraft in the night-fighter role. Mosquitos and Beaufighters had been obtained from the RAF under a kind of reverse Lend Lease. These aircraft were fitted with SCR-520 AI radars and assigned to several units in England. In the Pacific, several P-38Js were fitted with SCR-540 AI radars in an attempt to augment the aging Douglas P-70s.

This P-61A-1 (42-5488) on the ramp at Northrop Field in Hawthorne, California, was the third production Black Widow. The aircraft carried Yellow spinners and cowlings indicating it was a Northrop test aircraft. The P-61A differed from both the XP and YP-61 in the canopy shape and camouflage. Early production P-61As were delivered in Olive Drab over Neutral Gray undersides. (AFM)

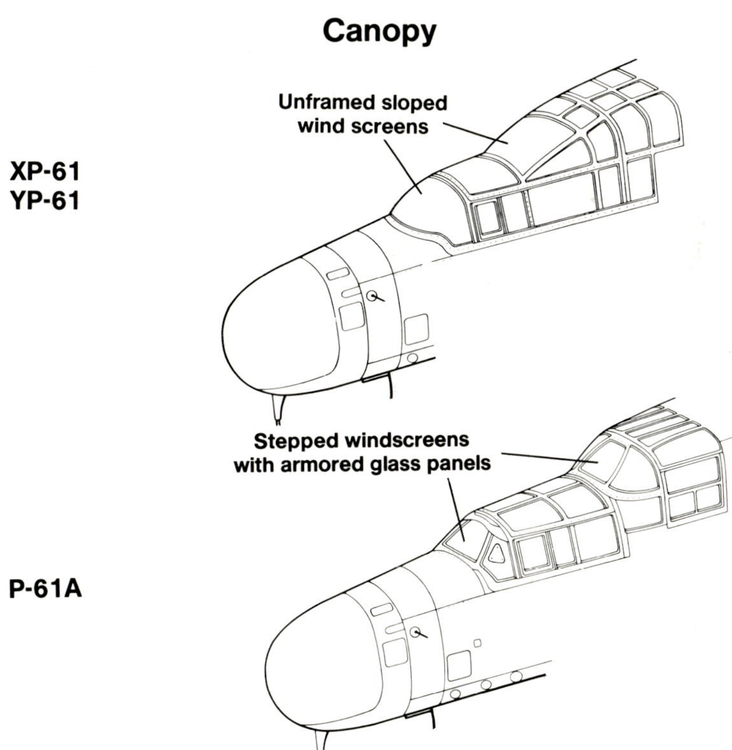

The first unit to take the P-61A into combat was the 6th Night-Fighter Squadron in Hawaii. The 6th NFS had been a night-fighter squadron since late 1942, flying Douglas P-70s and P-38J conversions. On 1 May 1944, the 6th NFS received its first P-61A Black Widow at Hickam Field, on Oahu. Once all the squadron's aircraft were assembled and checked out, the 6th began the long flight to Saipan. Two days later, the 419th NFS, based on Guadalcanal, exchanged its war-weary P-70s and P-38 conversions for P-61As.

In Europe, the first unit to take delivery of the P-61A was the 422nd NFS which had been trained at Orlando Field in YP-61s. On 9 May 1944, the 422nd brought their P-61As to Scorton RAF Station. They were followed a month later by the 425th NFS. Combat operations in both theaters began almost immediately, although it was the 6th NFS on Saipan that scored the first Black Widow kill.

One of the first units to begin operations from recently secured Isley Field on Saipan, the 6th NFS arrived on 21 June 1944. Nine days later, on 30 June, 2nd LT Dale Haberman and his radar operator (RO) Flight Officer (FO) Raymond Mooney intercepted two bogies in their P-61A *MOONHAPPY*. It took some thirty minutes for Mooney to vector the P-61 into position so that Haberman could make the kill. The bogies were identified as a Mitsubishi G4M Betty bomber with a Zero fighter escort. Haberman hit the Betty in the port engine, then dove the P-61A away from the Zero. Haberman later recalled, *"We left him like he was in reverse!"* The Betty was later seen exploding in the sea near Saipan.

The first European kill went to the 422nd NFS — but it was not a manned aircraft. On the night of 15/16 July 1944, LT Herman Ernst, with LT Edward Kopsel acting as RO, was vectored to intercept a German V-1 Buzz Bomb over the English Channel. LT Ernst brought his P-61A, *Borrowed Time* to within 900 feet of the flying bomb before he opened fire with his 20MM cannon, scoring hits on the V-1's propulsion unit. The robot went into a steep dive and exploded while still over the Channel.

The 422nd NFS introduced the use of Gloss Black as a camouflage for the P-61. The unit found that Gloss Black was a much better night scheme than either the Olive Drab/ Neutral Gray or Flat Black schemes. Flat Black paint absorbed light making the P-61 appear as a 'hole' in the glare of searchlights while Gloss Black reflected the searchlight beams. The light colored radome on some aircraft came from the unpainted fibreglass. Later the radomes were painted using RAF paints, most of which were light colors such as Yellow. When the aircraft were repainted Gloss Black, lead was often sprayed on the underside of the nose and radome to eliminate ground clutter, giving the nose a Light Gray color.

The 425th NFS decided to move the radar operator (RO) from the rear of the aircraft to the gunner's position behind the pilot. Even though the P-61As used by the 425th had no dorsal turrets, the gunner's seat was often retained for use by observers or for training other crew members. The 425th decided to move the RO into this vacant position in the aircraft. This would bring another pair of eyes into the cockpit which would greatly assist the pilot during night intruder missions.

9th Air Force brass originally vetoed the idea; however, one aircraft was modified "on the sly" and the results proved the concept. After flight testing the modified aircraft, 9th AF officials changed their minds and authorized the conversion for all turretless P-61As.

In the Pacific, aircraft of the 6th NFS were also field modified with four .50 caliber machine guns being mounted in the turret location, fixed to fire forward under the control of the pilot. The guns were given a standard turret cover and looked identical to a standard P-61A with a turret.

There were a number of high echelon Army officials that wanted to scrap the P-61 program and replace it with deHavilland Mosquito night-fighters. The Mosquito had been proven in combat by both RAF and USAAC crews and many felt that it was a superior aircraft to the P-61. American P-61 crews that already were flying the aircraft became upset and vocal about this possibility and some threatened to turn in their wings. As a result, an improvised flyoff was held on 5 July 1944 between a 422nd NFS P-61A and a Mosquito Mk 17 of No 125 Squadron, RAF.

The 422nd NFS official unit history recorded the results: *On the 5th, the long awaited test with a Mosquito (Mark 17) was laid on at 1600 local time. Squadron Leader Barnwell of 125 Squadron and his R/O flew the Mossie while LT Donald Doyle and F/O Norman Williams flew the Widow. The P-61 more than exceeded even our wildest hopes, being faster at 5,000, 10,000, 15,000, and 20,000 feet; it out-turned the Mossie at every altitude and by a big margin; and far surpassed the Mossie in rate of climb. We could go faster and slower up or down, faster than the pride of the British — it was a most enjoyable afternoon!* There were many, however, that believe that the Mosquito crew was told to lose so that Mosquitos that were badly needed by the RAF would not be diverted to the USAAF and so the P-61 would remain in service as a good, reliable night-fighter of American design.

This P-61A-1 (42-5528) of the 6th NFS at Kagman Point Field, Saipan, on 21 June 1944 carried the name *Jap Batty* on the nose in Yellow. Detachment B of the 6th NFS had seen combat at Guadalcanal flying modified P-38s and P-70s before converting to P-61As during May of 1944. The turret was replaced by a long range fuel tank for the flight to Saipan. (USAF via Jeff Ethell)

The first Black Widow to arrive in England was this P-61A-1 (42-5496), which was turned over to the RAF for testing at Boscombe Down. After evaluating the P-61 against both the Beaufighter and Mosquito, the RAF rejected the P-61A as being too slow. (AFM)

The pilot's cockpit of a P-61A. The empty square in the center of the instrument panel normally housed the pilot's radar scope. The windscreen panel directly in front of the pilot was of armored glass. (AFM)

The P-61A radar operator's station was equipped with a flexible light and a padded hood over the radar screen. (AFM)

Because of delays in the P-61 program, the Army Air Force was forced to use ex-Royal Air Force Bristol Beaufighters equipped with the SCR-520 airborne intercept (AI) radar to equip its night-fighter squadrons in Europe. This Beaufighter is assigned to the 416th NFS at Grottaglic, Italy during November of 1943. (AFM)

A P-61A (42-5508) of the 419th NFS flies over Guadalcanal during the Summer of 1944. The 419th was the second Pacific unit to convert to the P-61A. The rain, heat, blowing sand and dust in the Pacific caused extreme weathering on aircraft. (McDowell)

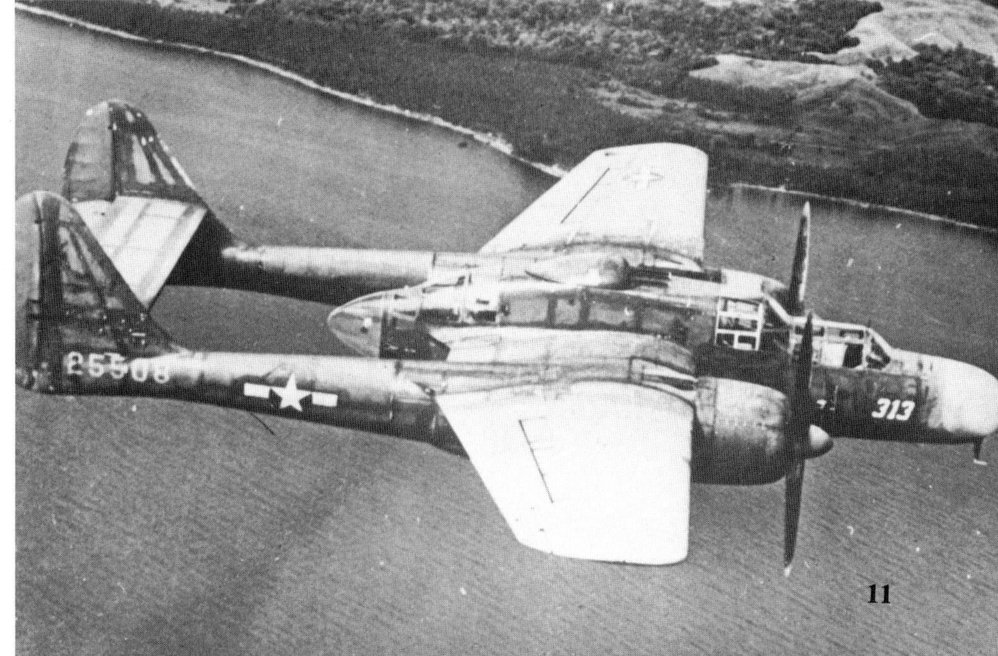

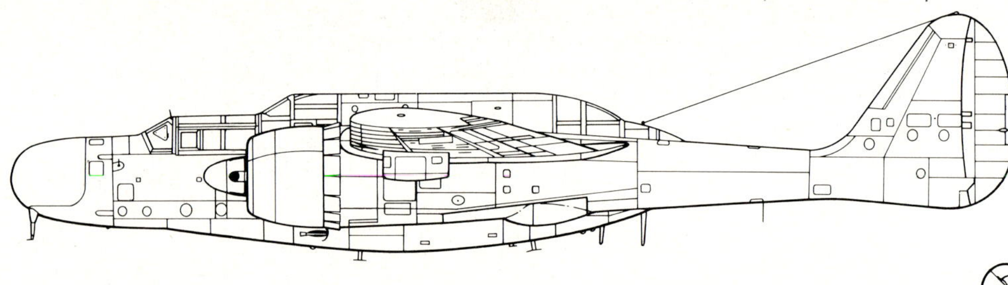

Specifications

Northrop P-61A Black Widow

Wingspan	66 feet
Length	48 feet 10 inches
Height	14 feet 2 inches
Empty Weight	20,965 pounds
Maximum Weight	32,400 pounds
Powerplants	Two 2,000 hp Pratt & Whitney R-2800-10/65 radial engines.
Armament	Four 20MM cannons and (when turret installed) four .50 caliber machine guns.
Performance	
Maximum Speed	372 mph
Service ceiling	34,000 feet
Range	1,210 miles
Crew	Three

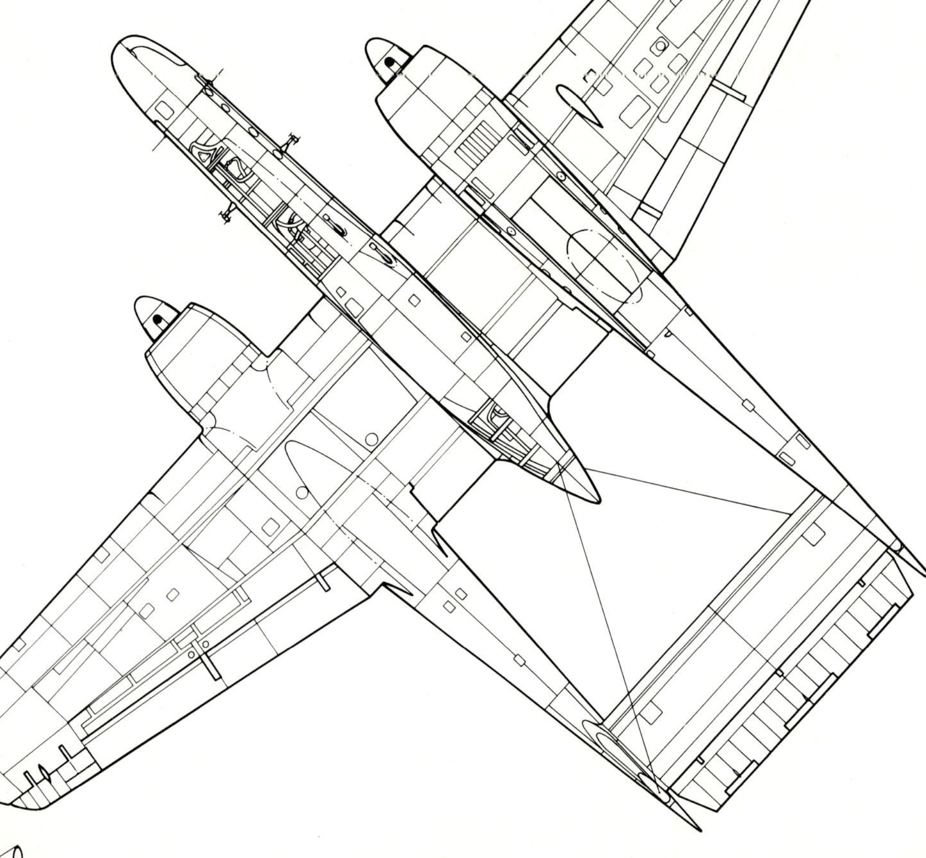

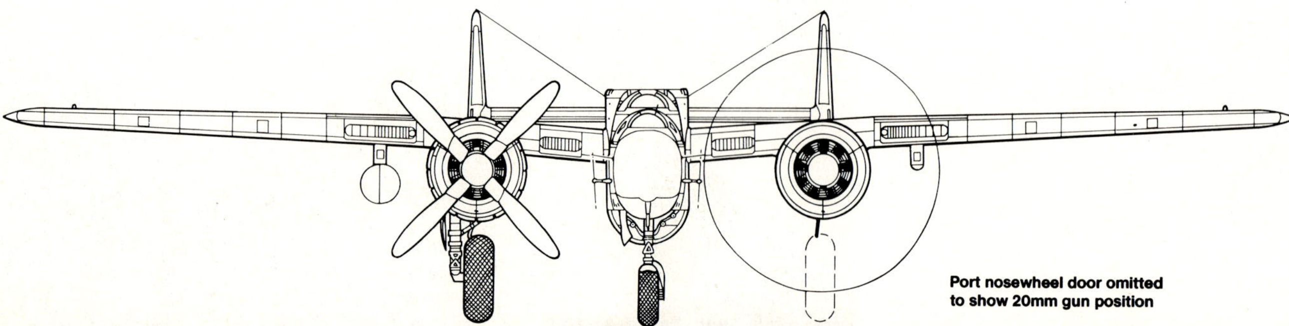

Port nosewheel door omitted to show 20mm gun position

Ground crews perform maintenance on the SCR-720 airborne intercept (AI) radar in the nose of a P-61A on Saipan during July of 1944. The radome was made of fiberglass and left unpainted, giving it a light color. (Dave McLaren)

LT Dale 'Hap' Haberman (right, pilot) and LT Ray Mooney (left, radar operator) scored the first Black Widow kill of the war in the Pacific when they shot down a Mitsubishi Betty on 30 June 1944 while flying their P-61A named *MOONHAPPY*. (Ernest Thomas)

This 6th NFS P-61A-1 has just arrived on Saipan and still has the ferry tank in the turret position. The tank was a modified B-24 bomb bay ferry tank that protruded above the fuselage of the P-61. Once the P-61 arrived at its base, the fuel tank was removed and replaced with either the turret or four forward firing .50 caliber guns. (Ernie McDowell)

"Midnight Mickey" was a P-61A-1 (42-5523) of the 6th NFS at Kagman Point Field (also known as East Field), Saipan. P-61 crews flew two hour patrols over Saipan from sunset to sunrise, with one aircraft being airborne at all times. (Northrop)

This P-61A (42-5488) on the ramp at Northrop Field was used by Northrop as a test aircraft and carried Yellow cowlings and the number 720. The aircraft was equipped with the standard GE Type A-4 four gun dorsal turret (AFM)

MAJ Emerson Barker, commander of the 419th NFS, taxis out to the active runway at Henderson Field on Guadalcanal. The 419th NFS used slanted three digit White numbers on the nose as their squadron marking. Barker's P-61A (42-5506) carried the number 311. (USAF via Jeff Ethell)

The Northrop test P-61A (42-5488, A/C number 720) was also flown with the four gun GE turret removed and was test flown to determine flight characteristics of the Widow without the turret. The aircraft has the large trailing edge flaps fully extended. (AFM)

Turret Installation

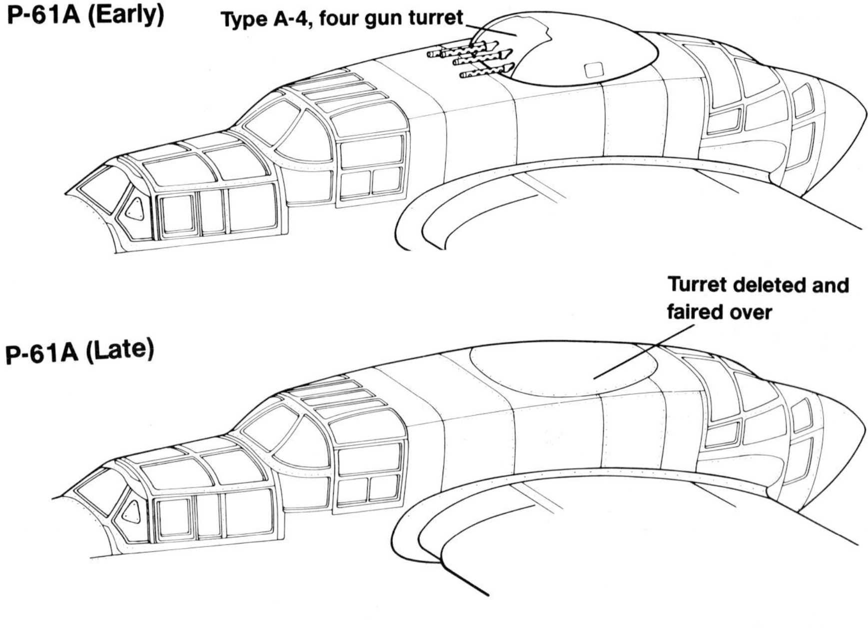

NIGHTIE MISSION was a P-61A-1 (42-5526) of the 6th NFS based at East Field, Saipan, during July of 1944. Although this aircraft was the 42nd P-61A built (the fifth aircraft after the dorsal turret was deleted), it retained the turret. Most 6th NFS aircraft were equipped with the turret. (Ernie McDowell)

This P-61A (42-5507) of the 419th NFS carried the number 312 on the nose in White. The squadron was based at Puerto Princesa on Palawan during 1944. The P-61As of 419th NFS were delivered in the early Olive Drab over Neutral Gray camouflage with clear Plexiglas radomes overpainted with a light coat of translucent paint on the inside of the dome. (Northrop)

The crew of *"Midnight Mickey"*, CAPT Myrle McCumber (pilot) and LT Daniel Hinz (radar operator) fill out the Form 1A paperwork after a mission. They had just finished painting the small Japanese flag under the cockpit representing the Mitsubishi G4M Betty bomber they shot down on 26 December 1944. (Ernest Thomas)

Most P-61s were delivered to the combat zones by ship, with their wings removed to make room on deck. This pair of P-61As of the 419th NFS were off loaded at Guadalcanal and towed up the causeway to Henderson Field where they were reassembled and made ready for combat. (AFM)

Armorers of the 6th NFS install four fixed forward firing .50 caliber machine guns in *Jap Batty* at Kagman Point Field, Saipan. A standard turret cover was placed over the guns to streamline them and, with the cover in place, the aircraft appeared identical to turret-equipped P-61As. (Dave McLaren)

A flight of four P-61s of the 6th NFS fly over the Pacific during early 1945. The aircraft in the foreground is *SLEEEPYTIME GAL II* flown by CAPT Ernest Thomas. (Crawford via Hernandez)

This P-61A, side number 321, was assigned to the 421st NFS at Tacloben Island. The 421st used small White 3 digit numbers on the tail and Yellow bands around the tail booms as their squadron identification markings. (Ernie McDowell)

Jap Batty was one of the first 6th Night Fighter Squadron P-61As to arrive on Saipan during June of 1944. She scored at least two kills while serving on Saipan. (Ernie McDowell)

A P-61A of the 421st NFS taxies to its parking spot on Biak Island during August of 1944. The 421st carried no identification markings on their P-61s. (via Bob Hernandez)

A White outline nude figure is carried on the nose of this P-61A based in the Pacific during 1945. Black Widow detachments served at various island bases throughout the Pacific area. (James Crow)

The *TACTLESS TEXAN* was a P-61A (42-5577) of the 422nd NFS. The Black Widow had the right wing tip and propeller damaged after the main landing gear collapsed on landing at Maupertus, France. The retractable ailerons are partially extended. (G. Stafford)

The pilot of this P-61A of the 422nd Night Fighter Squadron was too close to the V-1 Buzz Bomb he was firing on when it exploded. The P-61A flew through the fireball and had the fabric covering on the elevator and rudders nearly burned off. (G. Stafford)

BORROWED TIME was a P-61A (42-5547) of the 422nd NFS. LT Herman Ernst scored the first P-61 kill in the European Theater flying her on the night of 15/16 July 1944 when he destroyed a German V-1 Buzz Bomb while on a Anti-Diver Patrol over the English Channel. The mission markings are small lightning bolts and the kill marking is a small Red V-1. (AFM)

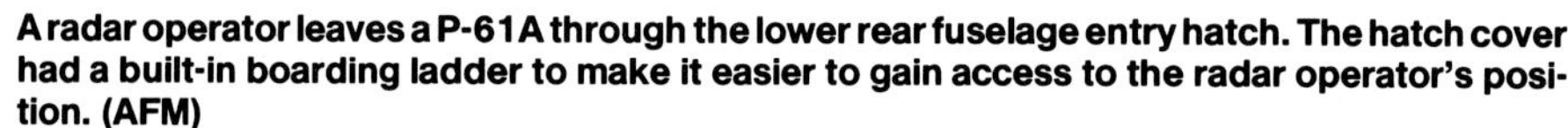

A radar operator leaves a P-61A through the lower rear fuselage entry hatch. The hatch cover had a built-in boarding ladder to make it easier to gain access to the radar operator's position. (AFM)

"Lady GEN" was the personal aircraft of LT Paul Smith, one of two P-61 pilots who scored five kills during the war. LT Smith shot down five German aircraft: an Me-410, an He-111, a Ju-88 and two Ju-188s. He also was credited with a V-1 Buzz Bomb and five German trains. Smith's radar operator was LT Robert Tierney.

These three P-61As of the 425th NFS over France during the Summer of 1944 all carry different camouflage schemes: *Husslin' Hussey*, a P-61A-5 (42-5536) is Olive Drab over Neutral Gray; *Lovely Lady*, P-61A-10 (42-5573) is overall Gloss Black with a painted radome and lead sprayed on the radome underside; and *Jukin' Judy*, P-61A-5 (42-5564) is overall Gloss Black with a Red and White sharkmouth. (Ernie McDowell)

Jukin Judy shares the ramp at Etain, France, with other P-61s of the 425th NFS during the Spring of 1945. The aircraft carried a sharkmouth and very faded D-Day stripes. (James Crow)

TENNESSEE "RIDGE RUNNER" was a P-61A of the 422nd NFS flown by CAPT John Anderson and LT James Morgan from Chateaudun, France during the Fall of 1944. (James Crow)

Maintenance crews use a twenty-four foot ladder to reach the wing of this P-61A of the 422nd NFS at Scorton, England during the Summer of 1944. (James Crow)

This overall Gloss Black P-61A of the 422nd NFS on the ramp at Scorton, England during June of 1944 carried full D-Day invasion stripes. Only two P-61 squadrons are known to have carried D-Day stripes — the 422nd and 425th Night Fighter Squadrons. (John Raths)

WACKY WABBIT crash landed at Florennes, Belgium during the Fall of 1944 after the port landing gear failed. She was later written off after another crash and the forward fuselage, nose and radome were mated to another P-61 named Midnite Wreck-Wizishin. (Gene Stafford)

LT Robert Bolinder flew *"DOUBLE TROUBLE"*, P-61A (42-5565), over France during the Summer of 1944. She was the first P-61A-10 off the Northrop assembly line and carried the name on the nose in White. LT Bolinder was credited with four kills: one Fw-190, one Me-110 and two He-111s. (Bob Bolinder)

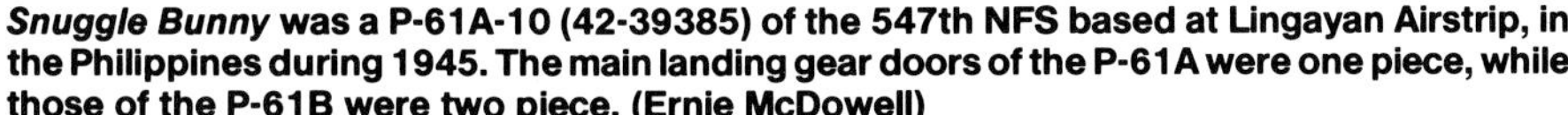
Snuggle Bunny was a P-61A-10 (42-39385) of the 547th NFS based at Lingayan Airstrip, in the Philippines during 1945. The main landing gear doors of the P-61A were one piece, while those of the P-61B were two piece. (Ernie McDowell)

LT Bob Bolinder's P-61A, *"DOUBLE TROUBLE"* carries a full set of D-Day invasion stripes. 8th Air Force orders purposely excluded night-fighters from the requirement of having to apply the Black and White recognition markings; however, someone forgot to notify the 422nd and 425th NFSs. (Bob Bolinder)

An unnamed nude female figure adorns the fuselage of this P-61A-11 (42-39378) of the 414th NFS at Furth, Germany, during the Summer of 1945. The Black Widow carried three kill and eight mission markings under the cockpit. (Chris Goodman)

This P-61A-10 (42-39349) was assigned to the 427th NFS at Myitkyina, Burma, during January of 1945. The aircraft had a very patchy appearance because of the way the paint weathered and peeled along every panel line joint. (Ken Summney via Jeff Ethell)

GEN Earl Barnes, Commander of the 13th Fighter Command, used this overall Natural Metal P-61A as his personal aircraft. The aircraft carried a B-24 bomb bay fuel tank in place of the dorsal turret and a football shaped ADF loop antenna housing under the rear fuselage. (Ernie McDowell)

TABITHA, a P-61A-10 (42-5569) of the 425th NFS, was parked on its hardstand at Coulommiers, France, during September of 1944. On 27 October 1944 the Black Widow crashed and was written off as a total loss. (USAF)

P-61B

During early 1944, a new and more powerful Airborne Intercept (AI) radar, the SCR-720C, became available for installation in the P-61. The new radar had an increased range of nearly 100 miles and a clearer image. Since the SCR-720C was larger than the earlier SCR-720A used in the P-61A, it was necessary to modify the Black Widow's nose section to house the new radar. As a result, the Army designated this variant of the Black Widow as the P-61B.

The P-61B differed primarily from the P-61A in the length of the nose section. The P-61B had an eight inch plug inserted in the fuselage just behind the radome. Additionally, the main landing gear doors were split, allowing the rear portion of the door to be closed after the main landing gear was down and locked. The door's actuators were changed from hydraulic to mechanical and a safety latch was added to the main landing gear retraction handle in the cockpit to eliminate the possibility of accidental gear retraction while the aircraft was on the ground.

The P-61B was also outfitted with another innovation known as "night binoculars" in the pilot's cockpit. These binoculars consisted of a pair of 5.8 power night glasses combined with the optical gunsight. A system of dots superimposed on the gunsight image allowed the pilot to determine the range of a target with greater accuracy. These "night binoculars" were also retrofitted to many P-61As already in service.

Other changes to the P-61B included a better crew heating system, automatic cowling cooling flaps, an additional taxi light installed on the nosewheel strut, the aileron trim tabs were deleted, and fire extinguishers were built into the engine nacelles. The four gun dorsal turret was not installed, although all wiring and fittings were installed. The first P-61B rolled out during July of 1944.

There were various changes and improvements made to the P-61B during its production run. These changes included a low altitude altimeter, two additional underwing pylons installed inboard of the engine nacelles (capable of carrying either drop tanks or bombs) and an APS-13 Tail Warning Radar (beginning with the P-61B-10). At Block -15, the General Electric Type A-4 dorsal turret was reintroduced. Later, a new turret, the A-7, was introduced on Block -20 aircraft. There were seven Block -25 aircraft built, which were strictly testbeds for the new Western Electric APG-1 Gun Laying Radar/GE remote controlled dorsal turret.

During the Summer of 1944, P-61s began flying night intruder missions. With the Allies having total air superiority during daylight, the Germans were forced to move rail and truck traffic under the cover of darkness. 9th Air Force P-61 crews were ordered to conduct night ground attack missions using their radar to detect targets such as trains and truck convoys. Sometimes napalm was used to stop a train or truck convoy, then the P-61 crew would use the light of the fire to attack the convoy repeatedly with their cannons. Several aircraft in the 425th NFS were modified to carry five inch Bazooka rocket tubes under the wings to increase their air-to-ground fire power. P-61s, operating in the night intruder role, were very effective during the Battle of the Bulge, scoring seven night aircraft kills in addition to destroying large amounts of rolling stock and a number of locomotives. Typical armament for intruder missions was a pair of 500 pound bombs or napalm tanks and rockets.

In the Pacific Theater, P-61s were also used in the night intruder role and several aircraft of the 427th NFS were modified with underwing Bazooka rocket tubes, while others were modified with five inch zero length rocket stubs under the outboard wing panels. In addition to their P-61Bs, the 418th NFS used several B-25H bombers for the intruder missions. Initially, the aircraft retained the 75MM cannon armament, but it was later removed when it was found that the muzzle blast almost blinded the crew. The 418th's B-25Hs were painted Flat Black and carried the same markings as the 418th's P-61s.

The nose of the P-61B was extended some eight inches between the radome and the cockpit to make room for the larger, more powerful SCR-720C radar. This P-61B (42-39454) was eventually issued to the 548th NFS and was named *Cooper's Snooper*. (AFM)

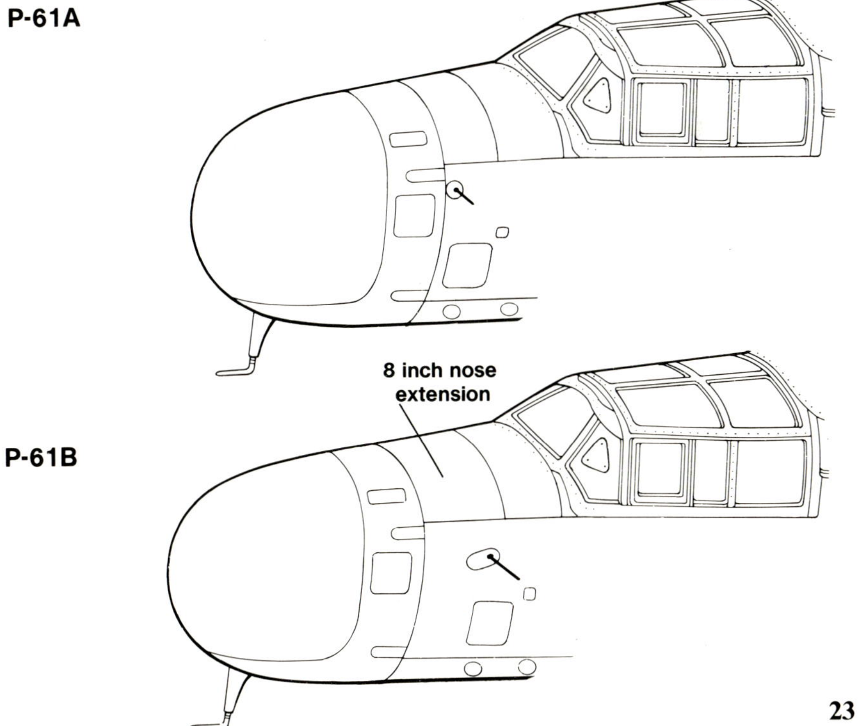

One of the changes between the P-61A and P-61B was the addition of a landing and steering light mounted on the nose gear strut. (USAF)

Normal routine for a P-61 crew was two nights on alert (you slept during the day) and two nights off. Since there had to be a P-61 in the air at all times during the hours of darkness, the airborne alert aircraft could not land until the ground alert aircraft was airborne. Alert crews were assigned specific combat air patrol hours covering the period of sunset to sunrise. Crews would pre-flight their aircraft during the late afternoon while wearing dark Red goggles. These goggles acclimated their eyes to the dark and improved their night vision. A normal Combat Air Patrol usually lasted two hours and they were usually very boring. There were those missions, however, that weren't.

CAPT Ernest Thomas of the 548th NFS relates one such mission.

We were airborne on a regular CAP at 1830 and spent an uneventful two hours. Just as we were about to start for home at 2030, Agate 9 (Saipan GCI radar) notified us that there were Bogies coming from the north. At about 2049, we had closed to minimum range, but with flaps down, throttles closed, and flying less than 95 mph, I could not stay behind the Bogie. As I overshot, Corporal Tew -my Gunner - got a visual with his binoculars. It was a Jap Betty bomber. After several tries, I still could not keep the aircraft behind the Betty and finally stalled out. After recovery, neither my crew nor Agate 9 could locate the Bogie.

Very shortly after, Agate 9 put us on another Bogie going south. After closing to minimum range, Corporal Tew identified it as another Betty. I overshot this Betty three times, each time going a full 360 degrees to pick him up again. The Betty had evidently seen us and was trying to run as he was picking up speed. On my fourth intercept, the Betty was up to 19,000 feet and indicating 155 mph. This time I closed on him and remained behind him without difficulty. I got my visual at 1,200 feet.

The Betty pilot apparently saw me, as he started a hard turn to the left. We closed to within 600 feet, where I was able to pull the gunsight through the Betty for a deflection shot. My first burst (thirty-two rounds of 20MM and thirty-eight rounds of .50 caliber) hit his left engine, which exploded immediately and burst into flames. I broke hard right and passed under the burning plane, missing it by about 200 feet. Orbiting to the

Landing/Steering Light

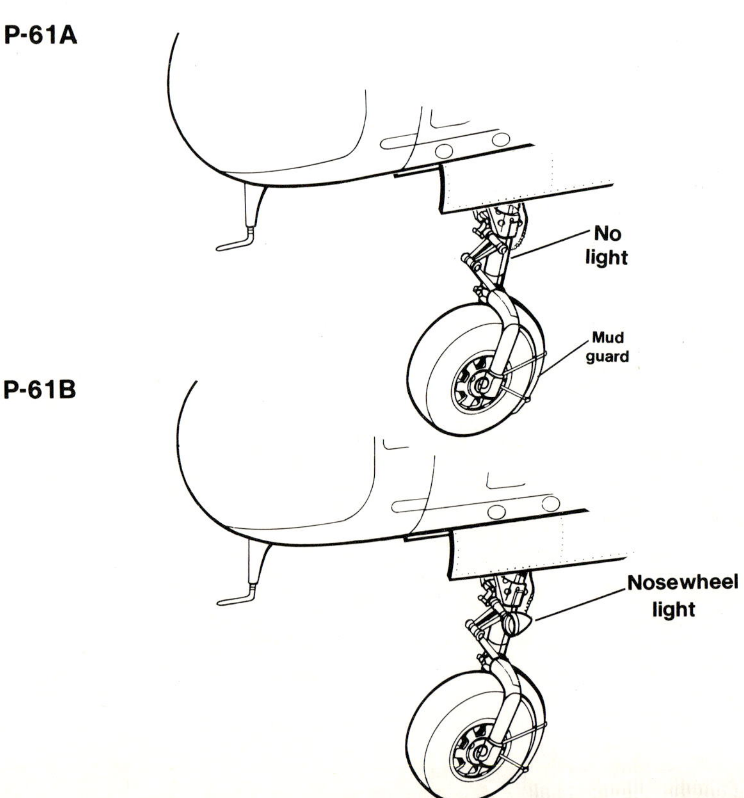

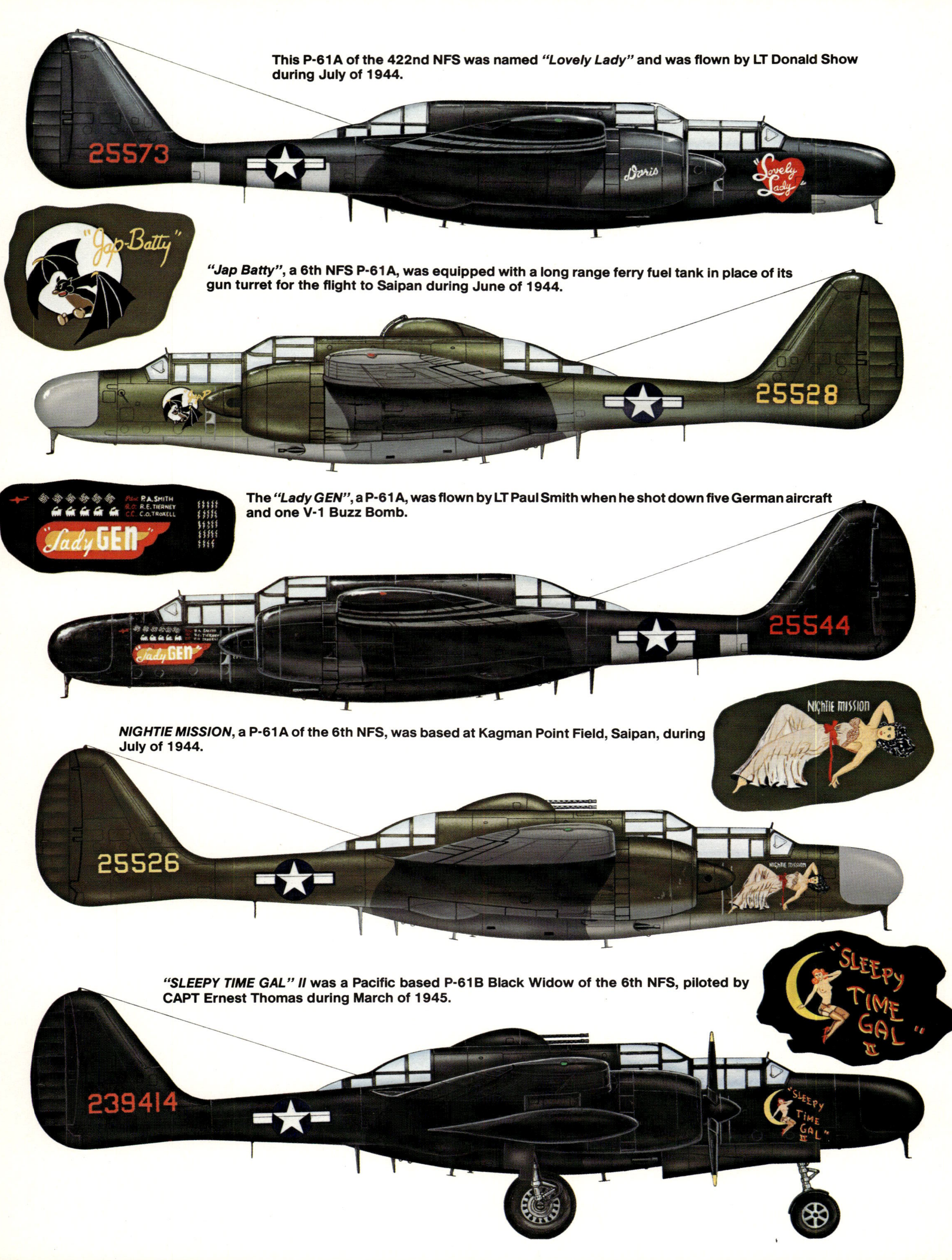

This P-61A of the 422nd NFS was named *"Lovely Lady"* and was flown by LT Donald Show during July of 1944.

"Jap Batty", a 6th NFS P-61A, was equipped with a long range ferry fuel tank in place of its gun turret for the flight to Saipan during June of 1944.

The *"Lady GEN"*, a P-61A, was flown by LT Paul Smith when he shot down five German aircraft and one V-1 Buzz Bomb.

NIGHTIE MISSION, a P-61A of the 6th NFS, was based at Kagman Point Field, Saipan, during July of 1944.

"SLEEPY TIME GAL" II was a Pacific based P-61B Black Widow of the 6th NFS, piloted by CAPT Ernest Thomas during March of 1945.

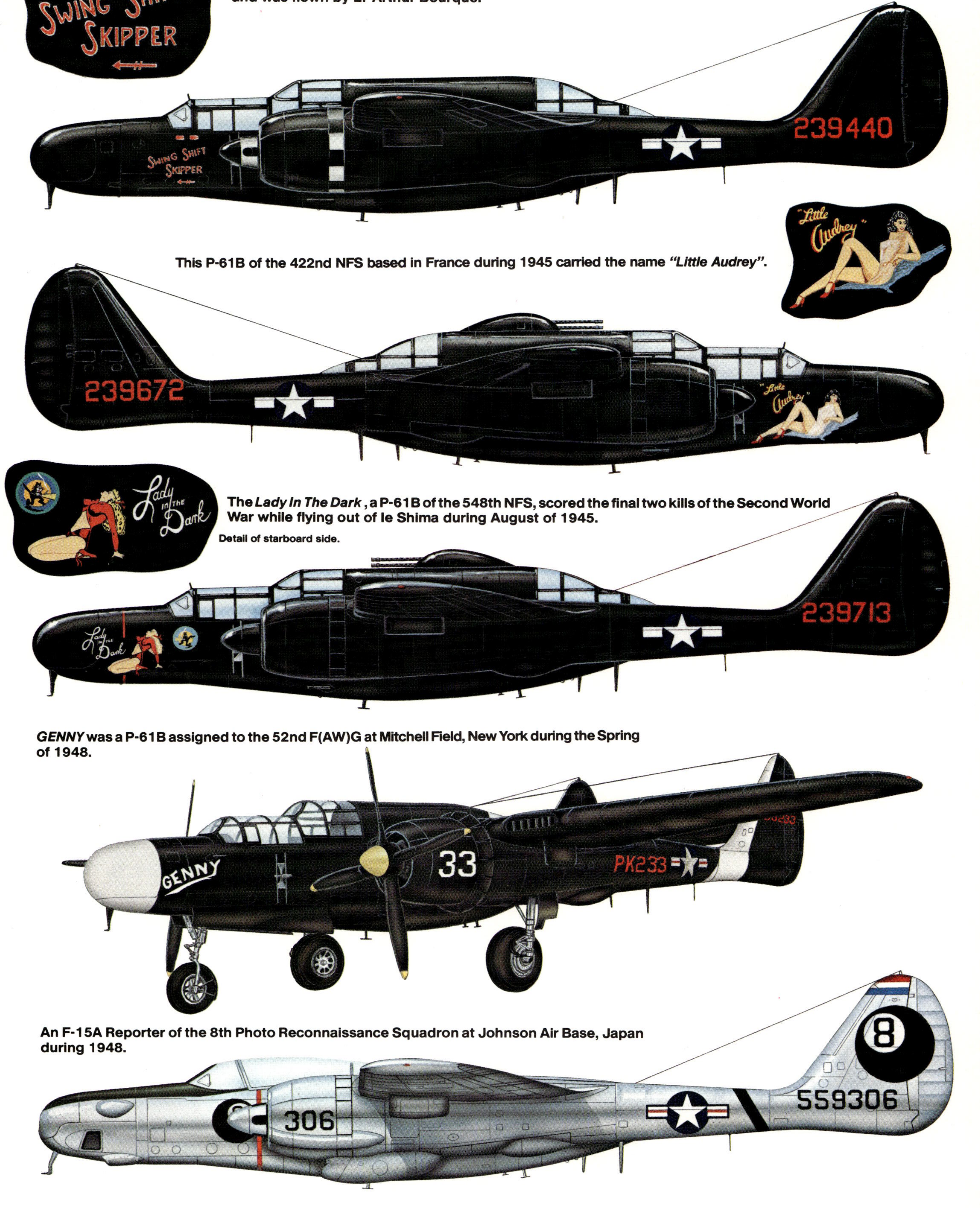

SWING SHIFT SKIPPER, a P-61B of the 547th NFS was based at Lingayen Airstrip, Philippines and was flown by LT Arthur Bourque.

This P-61B of the 422nd NFS based in France during 1945 carried the name ***"Little Audrey"***.

The *Lady In The Dark*, a P-61B of the 548th NFS, scored the final two kills of the Second World War while flying out of Ie Shima during August of 1945.

Detail of starboard side.

GENNY was a P-61B assigned to the 52nd F(AW)G at Mitchell Field, New York during the Spring of 1948.

An F-15A Reporter of the 8th Photo Reconnaissance Squadron at Johnson Air Base, Japan during 1948.

right, I watched the Betty go down. A few seconds later, the whole sky was lit up by a large explosion. There was nothing where the Betty had been but a large glow below the cloud deck. Agate 9 vectored us back to the base, about 95 miles away, and we pancaked on Saipan at 2235. This CAP had lasted over four hours.

By the end of the Second World War, the Army Air Force had fifteen of its sixteen night-fighter squadrons equipped with Northrop P-61As or P-61Bs. The last squadron to convert to the Black Widow was the 416th NFS, which exchanged its deHavilland Mosquito NF Mk 30s for P-61Bs during the Summer of 1945.

It was a P-61B that scored the last kill of the Second World War. On the night of 14/15 August 1945, a 548th NFS P-61B named *Lady In The Dark*, flown by LT Robert Clyde, with LT Bruce Leford as his RO, forced a Nakajima Ki-43 Oscar into the sea near Ie Shima. Although the war had officially ended at 0800 on 15 August 1945, the "Lady" got a second kill the night of 15/16 August when CAPT (Solie) Soloman, with LT John Scheerer as RO, forced a Ki-44 Tojo into the Pacific. Two kills without ever firing a shot! The last operational combat unit to fly the P-61 was the 68th F(AW)S, which had at least one F-61B on strength as late as May of 1950. Six weeks after completing its conversion to F-82 Twin Mustangs, the unit was involved in combat over Korea.

FT-1/F2T-1

The Northrop FT-1 was actually a P-61B redesignated by the Navy for use by the Marine Corps. FT-1s were a mixed bag of twelve P-61Bs (BuNos 52750 to 52761) that were transferred to the Marine Corps during September of 1945. These were used to help train Marine night-fighter crews in radar intercept tactics before they converted to the Grumman F7F Tigercat night-fighter. The FT-1s were unarmed, ex-trainer aircraft from Hammer Field, California, the Army night-fighter training base.

Later, the aircraft were re-designated as F2T-1s. Marine training operations ceased on 1 May 1946, with the aircraft being reassigned to Marine Corps Air Stations Cherry Point and El Toro. On 31 August 1947, the last F2T-1 was retired from the Navy inventory.

Crews bore-sight all eight guns of a P-61B into the firing butts at a fighter base. The 20MM cannons were harmonized to converge at 300 yards, the .50 caliber machine guns were set to converge at 600 yards. (Northrop)

The pilot's instrument panel on a P-61B. The small square in the center of the panel is the pilot's radar scope and the object in the center above the panel is the reflector gun sight. (Jeff Ethell)

Black Widow units also flew night intruder missions, such as train-busting, when airborne targets became scarce. This P-61B of the 427th NFS at Myitkyina, Burma, during 1944 is armed with six 5 inch bazooka rocket launcher tubes under the wings for air-to-ground missions. (AFM)

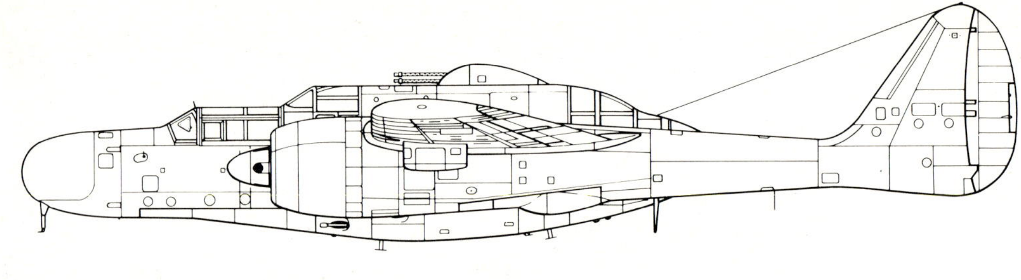

Specifications

Northrop P-61B Black Widow

Wingspan .... 66 feet
Length .... 49 feet 6 inches
Height .... 14 feet 8 inches
Empty Weight .... 27,000 pounds
Maximum Weight .... 38,000 pounds
Powerplants .... Two 2,000 hp Pratt & Whitney R-2800-65 radial engines.

Armament .... Four 20MM cannon and four .50 caliber machine guns.

Performance
Maximum Speed .... 366 mph
Service ceiling .... 33,100 feet
Range .... 1,010 miles
Crew .... Two or three

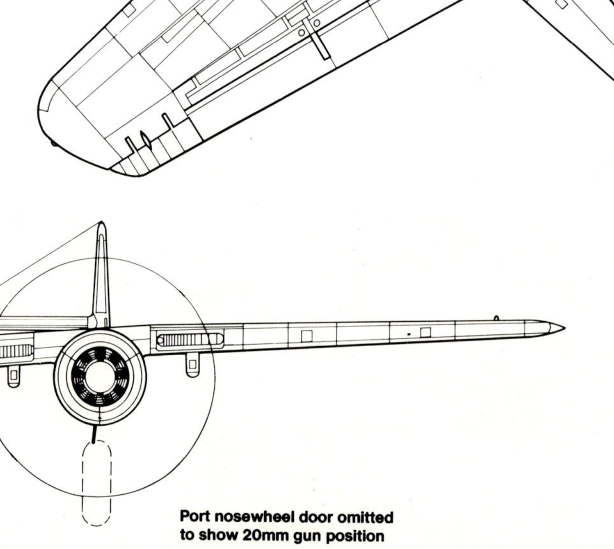

Port nosewheel door omitted to show 20mm gun position

A new production P-61B-15 on a test flight over Southern California during the Summer of 1945. The Gloss Black camouflage proved to be more effective than the earlier Flat Black since Gloss Black reflected light while Flat Black absorbed light. (Ernie McDowell)

FIRST NIGHTER was a P-61B of the 414th NFS based at Strassfeld, Germany, during 1945. The longer nose on the P-61B made the fuselage appear more slender and longer than it actually was. (Merle Olmsted)

The P-61's Gloss Black paint easily peeled from the leading edges of the wings, stabilizers and the front of the engine cowlings like the paint on *THE BEAUTIFUL ASS,* a P-61B of the 414th NFS. The 414th received their first P-61Bs in December of 1944. (USAF via Jeff Ethell)

LT Milt Green's *BLIND DATE*, a P-61B of the 549th NFS, on patrol over the island of Iwo Jima during 1945. The *DATE* was a late production P-61B-15 with the dorsal turret, and underwing pylons capable of carrying either drop tanks or bombs. (Milt Green)

The General Electric Type A-4 remote control dorsal turret was armed with four Browning M2 .50 caliber machine guns. The guns are at maximum elevation and the flexible ammunition feeds are fully loaded. (Northrop)

Sand and dirt driven by the violent winds of a Pacific typhoon sandblasted the paint completely off the rear fuselage and booms of this P-61B of the 418th NFS. The national insignia has been repainted. (AFM)

LT Mel Bode tried to land *The SPOOK* in a rare heavy fog on Iwo Jima. The left wingtip struck the ground, the Black Widow hit another P-61 and finally came to a halt 150 feet later. The impact of the crash set off all four cannons, which kept firing until they finally ripped completely out of the aircraft. (Northrop)

SGT Lawrence Lambert, the first American to test an ejection seat, climbs into the test aircraft, a P-61B (42-39498) named *Jack In The Box*. The test held on 17 August, 1946, was completely successful. (USAF via David H. Klaus)

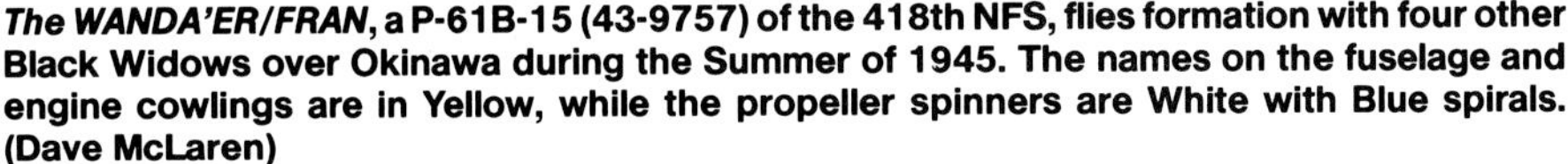
The WANDA'ER/FRAN, **a P-61B-15 (43-9757) of the 418th NFS, flies formation with four other Black Widows over Okinawa during the Summer of 1945. The names on the fuselage and engine cowlings are in Yellow, while the propeller spinners are White with Blue spirals. (Dave McLaren)**

The artist puts the finishing touches to *"LITTLE AUDREY,"* a P-61B-15 (42-39672) of the 422nd Night-Fighter Squadron at Florennes, Belgium, during the Spring of 1945. (AFM)

Ground crews refuel *BLACK MAGIC* a P-61B-15 of the 414th Night-Fighter Squadron at Pantedora, Italy, during 1945. The aircraft was flown by Rip Bolender. (AFM)

This overall Gloss Black P-61B of the 422nd Night-Fighter Squadron parked on the Marston matting at its forward base in France during 1945, carried the name *"LITTLE AUDREY"* on the nose.

Four P-61Bs of the 548th NFS line the ramp on Ie Shima on 10 March 1945. The aircraft had Red propeller spinners, cowl flaps, and a Red stripe around the nose. (Ernie McDowell)

A pair of P-61B-15s of the 414th NFS fly over the Mediterranean Sea. The light colored areas above the wings are heavy exhaust stains, common on all P-61 variants. (Ernie McDowell)

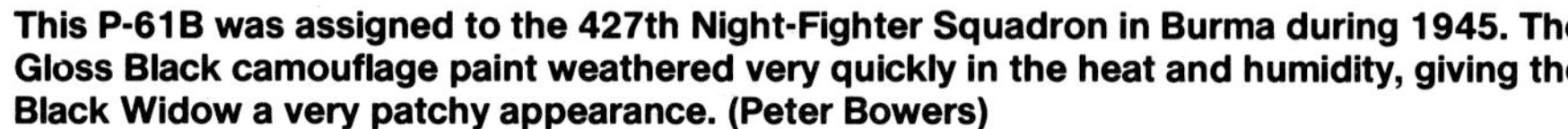

This P-61B was assigned to the 427th Night-Fighter Squadron in Burma during 1945. The Gloss Black camouflage paint weathered very quickly in the heat and humidity, giving the Black Widow a very patchy appearance. (Peter Bowers)

Main Landing Gear Doors

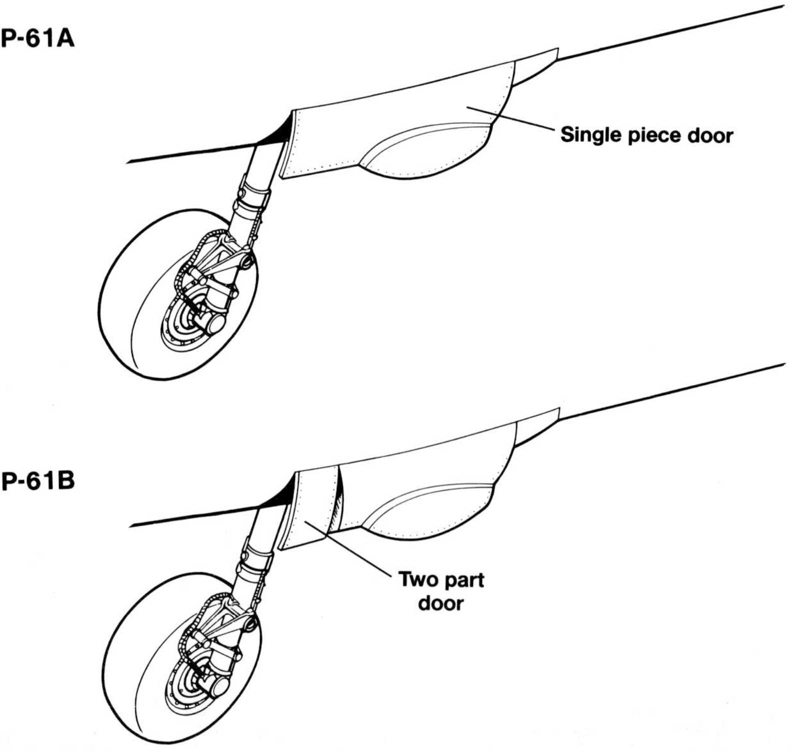

Lady in the Dark was a P-61B of the 548th NFS based on Ie Shima during 1945. *Lady* scored the last kill of the Second World War.

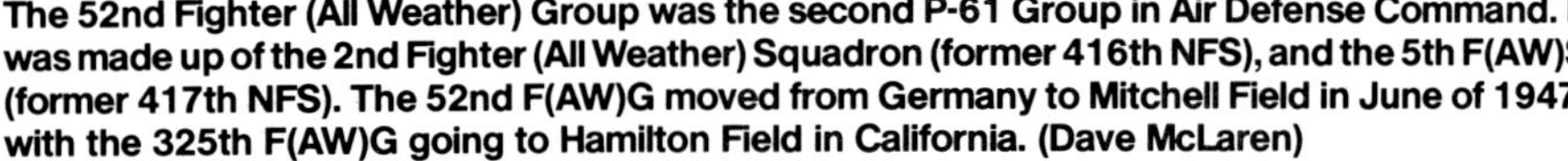

The 52nd Fighter (All Weather) Group was the second P-61 Group in Air Defense Command. It was made up of the 2nd Fighter (All Weather) Squadron (former 416th NFS), and the 5th F(AW)S (former 417th NFS). The 52nd F(AW)G moved from Germany to Mitchell Field in June of 1947, with the 325th F(AW)G going to Hamilton Field in California. (Dave McLaren)

Probably the most famous Black Widow was *Lady In The Dark* of the 548th NFS. The *Lady* was credited with the last two kills of the Second World War. Both kills were achieved without firing a shot when the P-61 forced both Japanese fighters into the sea.

Trim Tabs

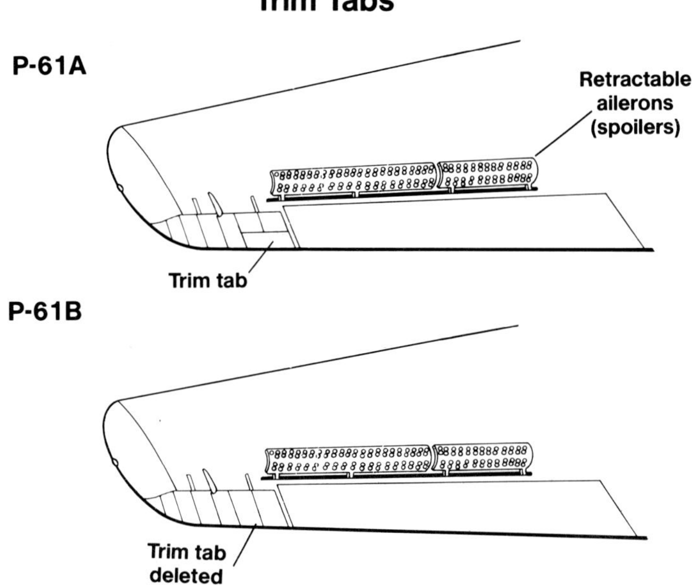

Ground crews position *LITTLE TEXAS KING*, a P-61B-20 (43-8275) of the 52nd F(AW)G, on the ramp at Mitchell Field, New York. In addition to the White nose, 52nd aircraft had White stripes on the tail boom. None of the 52nd aircraft carried dorsal turrets. (Dave McLaren)

My Joan, an F-61B of the 339th F(AW)S on the ramp at Misawa, Japan during 1949. By 1949 only a few F-61s remained in service with the Far East Air Force and these were rapidly being replaced by F-82 Twin Mustangs. (Mike Zeljak)

An F-61B-20 (43-8278) of the 325th F(AW)G on the ramp of its home base, Hamilton Air Force Base, California. The two squadrons within the 325th, the 317th and 318th F(AW)Ss, transitioned to the F-82F just prior to moving to bases in Washington state. The PK buzz number stood for — P for Pursuit aircraft and K for Northrop P-61. (Stan Staples)

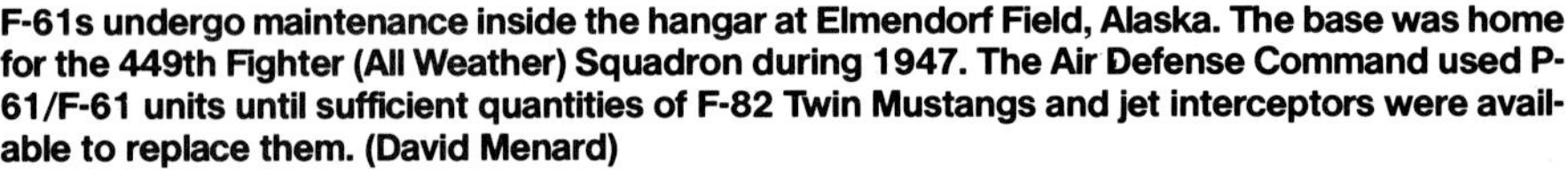

F-61s undergo maintenance inside the hangar at Elmendorf Field, Alaska. The base was home for the 449th Fighter (All Weather) Squadron during 1947. The Air Defense Command used P-61/F-61 units until sufficient quantities of F-82 Twin Mustangs and jet interceptors were available to replace them. (David Menard)

The 325th F(AW)G became operational with P-61Bs at Mitchell Field, New York during May of 1947, then was transferred to Hamilton Field, California. The 325th Group consisted of three squadrons, two of which were equipped with P-61s. This 318th F(AW)S P-61B-20 is making an approach to Hamilton Field during early 1948. (Gene Yagan)

The U.S. Marine Corps obtained twelve P-61Bs during September 1945 directly from the Army training command and designated them as F2T-1s. They were used to train Marine air crews in night fighter tactics before they received their first Grumman F7F Tigercat night fighters. The F2T-1s were phased out by August of 1947. (AFM)

This crashed P-61B was being recovered by members of the Mid-Atlantic Air Museum from the mountains of Indonesia during March of 1989. The aircraft was successfully recovered and is awaiting restoration. It is hoped that the P-61B will be returned to flying status. (MAAM via Russell Strine)

This P-61B is in the Red Chinese Air Force museum in Beijing, China and is one of two P-61Bs known to still exist. The aircraft is currently for sale with an asking price of $2 million. (Northrop)

P-61C

Both the P-61A and P-61B were felt to have a deficiency in top speed and operational service ceiling and the Army sought to improve both these areas of performance by installing turbo-supercharged engines on the P-61. On 11 November 1943, the Army Air Force authorized the Air Technical Service Command and Northrop to begin development of a high performance P-61 under the designation XP-61C. The XP-61C would be powered by turbo-supercharged 2,800 hp Pratt & Whitney R-2800C engines. With this increase in power, the XP-61C was estimated to have a top speed of near 430 mph at an altitude of 30,000 feet.

With Northrop heavily involved in production of both P-61As and the Vengeance, in addition to development work on the XB-35 Flying Wing bomber program, a subcontractor was needed to do the modification on the P-61A airframes selected for conversion to the XP-61C configuration. Goodyear Aircraft in Akron, Ohio, was selected and a pair of P-61As were delivered to the company. The XP-61C was to be powered by R-2800-27 engines; however, Army demands for these engines were so heavy that Goodyear had to install R-2800-14W engines (the Navy equivalent). By the time the two aircraft were ready for testing, they were powered by still a third engine type, the R-2800-57. On 27 April 1944, the Army redesignated both aircraft as XP-61Ds.

The Army envisioned that the two XP-61D prototypes would serve as the test aircraft for the production variant which would be designated the P-61C. Goodyear faced a number of problems with the program, not the least of which was Northrop's inability to help because of the priority placed on the XB-35 program. Most of the problems centered around the engines. The piston clearances were too strict and had to be opened up, exhaust gases from the turbo-supercharger gates burned the bottom of the engine nacelle leading to a redesign of the gate. Finally, the aircraft were once again re-engined when the proposed production power plants, the R-2800-77s, finally arrived.

Flight tests proved that the performance of the XP-61D was what the Army expected and the aircraft was ordered into production (Contract W535 ac-29319 for 207 aircraft) under the designation P-61C. The first production P-61C rolled off the Hawthorne assembly line during July of 1945. The production contract was later amended to six P-61B-25s and 201 P-61Cs. The performance of the P-61C led the Army to place additional production orders bringing the total to over 400 P-61Cs. With the end of the Second World War, however, these orders were cancelled and the P-61C production line was shut down. A total of fifty-four P-61Cs were built, thirteen of which were scrapped right off the assembly line.

The P-61C differed from the P-61B in the engine nacelle, propellers and in the use of "fighter brakes" in place of the wing spoilers. The P-61C had a redesigned engine nacelle and cowling with air intakes on each side of the cowling for the carburetors. The supercharger was housed in a large bulged fairing under the nacelle. The P-61C replaced the earlier Hamilton Standard narrow chord four blade propellers with A.O. Smith four blade wide chord (paddle blade) propellers.

The "fighter brakes" were large, perforated hydraulically operated panels fitted on both the upper and lower outer wing panels in front of the wing flaps. These deployed into the airstream over the wing, similar to the way a speed/dive brake was used. The "fighter brakes," however, were also used to increase the aircraft's rate of turn, allowing the P-61C to turn much tighter than either the P-61A or P-61B and avoid overshooting targets. The armament, radar and other electronics was the same as a late production P-61B.

Performance of the P-61C was greatly improved over previous P-61 variants — maximum speed rose from 370 mph to 430 mph and the service ceiling went from 33,000 feet to 41,000 feet.

With the end of the war, however, the P-61C was not used in its intended role. Besides the twelve aircraft that were briefly assigned to the Air Defense Command at McChord Field outside Seattle, Washington, the majority of P-61Cs were relegated to research and test missions. The biggest of these was the thunderstorm research program conducted under Air Material Command. The mission of Project THUNDERSTORM was to penetrate thunderstorms at various altitudes and take instrument readings. A number of P-61Cs were also used for test missions with NACA and the Navy. A few were used as chase aircraft at Northrop for various Northrop aircraft projects. By April of 1949, however, all P-61Cs had been stricken from the active Air Force inventory.

The XP-61C, later redesignated the XP-61D, was a P-61A re-engined with 2,800 hp turbo-supercharged Pratt & Whitney R-2800-77 engines. Two prototypes were built, both being finished in overall Natural Metal with Yellow engine cowlings. (Northrop)

One of the distinctive features of the P-61C was fighter brakes that replaced the Northrop Retractable ailerons, used on all earlier P-61 variants. Reportedly, the fighter brakes kept the aircraft from overshooting targets on an intercept and also enabled the P-61C to turn tighter than any earlier Black Widow. (Northrop)

Fighter Brakes

P-61C

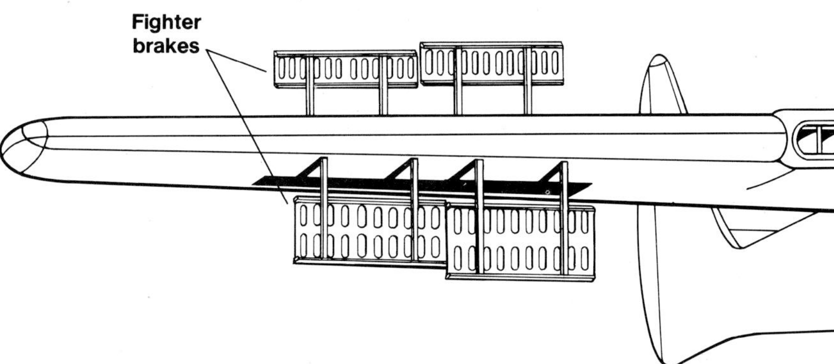

Several production P-61Cs were used by active Army or Air Force units. This P-61C-1 (43-8351) was assigned to the 325th F(AW)G at Hammer Field. Although P-61Cs were delivered with A-7 dorsal turrets, by 1948 these had been deleted to save weight. (USAF via David Menard)

The pilot of this P-61C (43-8339) of the 449th F(AW)S, stationed at Ladd Field, Alaska, ground looped the aircraft on landing. The aircraft has been stripped of all usable parts and parked in the aircraft junkyard at Ladd waiting to be scrapped. (L. Coombs via Jeff Ethell)

This P-61C was one of the black Widows used during Project THUNDERSTORM. The aircraft were assigned to Air Material Command and were flown into and through violent weather to determine the effects on aircraft. The nose flash is Red and Yellow as are the wingtip and tail markings, while the cowl ring was Yellow and the spinners were Red.(David Menard)

This F-61C was assigned to Hammer Field, California as a night-fighter trainer, preparing pilots for the F-82 Twin Mustang program. The de-icer boots have been removed from the leading edges of all the flying surfaces and the dorsal turret has been deleted and the opening faired over. (USAF)

Cowling

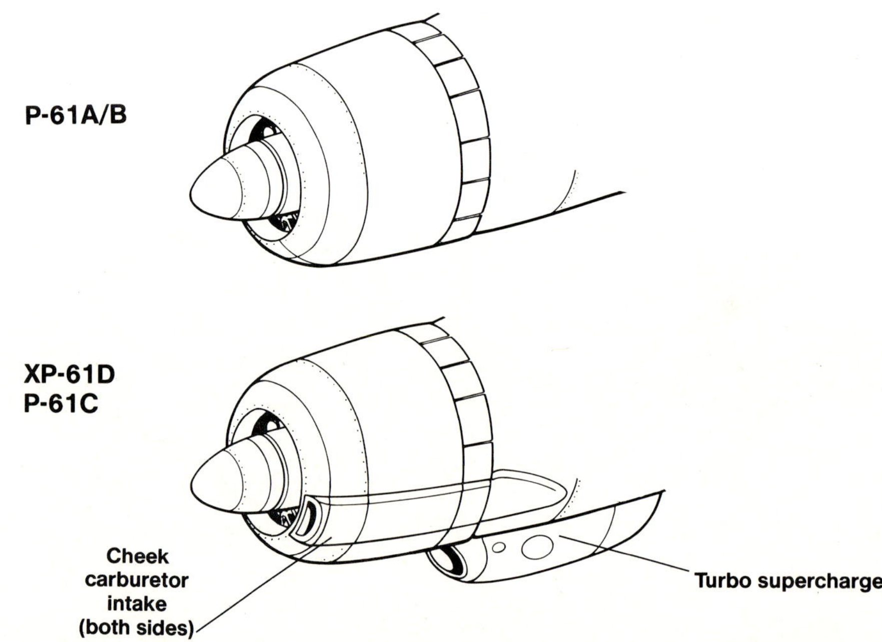

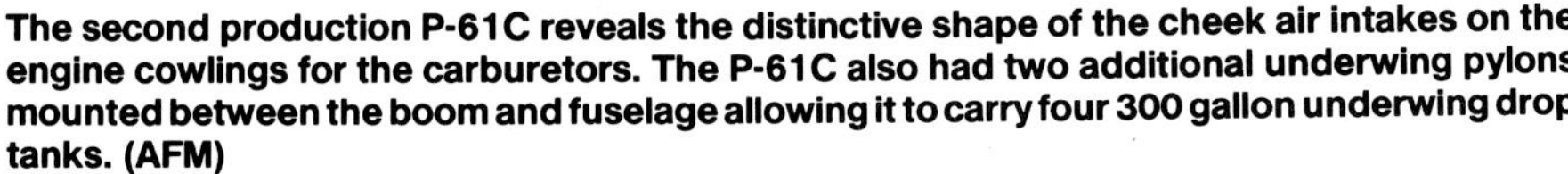

The second production P-61C reveals the distinctive shape of the cheek air intakes on the engine cowlings for the carburetors. The P-61C also had two additional underwing pylons mounted between the boom and fuselage allowing it to carry four 300 gallon underwing drop tanks. (AFM)

One of the two surviving P-61Cs parked on the Air Force Museum ramp at Wright Patterson Air Force Base, Ohio. The aircraft has been repainted and currently carries the markings of *Moonlight Serenade* of the 550th NFS. P-61Cs did not see combat. (Jim Sullivan)

The second production P-61C-1 (43-8322) was used as a chase aircraft for the advanced XB-35 Flying Wing project. The XB-35 was later re-engined with jet power plants and became the XB-49. (AFM)

Propeller

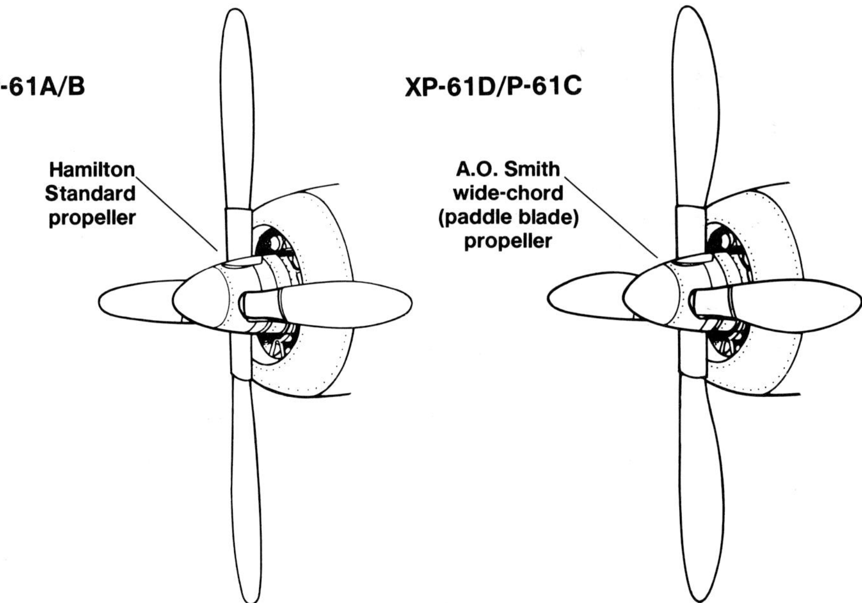

XP-61E

The XP-61E was Northrop's answer to an Army Air Force requirement for a long range, day, escort fighter with the proposed mission of long range fighter escort of B-29 bombers to Moscow. The Army and Northrop had first discussed the possibility of a day-fighter variant of the P-61 as early as the Spring of 1944, and GEN George Kinney and members of the 5th Air Force staff had talked with Northrop's John Myers about just such an aircraft during the Summer of 1944 (for long range escort missions to Japan). Although Army officials at Air Material Command were against such a project, the Army amended the XP-61D prototype contract to include two XP-61E day-fighter prototypes. Two P-61B-10s were pulled from the Hawthorne production line in October of 1944 to be modified into the day-fighter configuration.

The XP-61E was basically a late production P-61B with a highly modified fuselage. The cockpit area was redesigned with the turret, gunner's cockpit and radar operator's position being deleted. The cockpit of the XP-61E housed the crew of two in tandem under a large bubble canopy. The SCR-720C nose-mounted AI radar was replaced by four .50 caliber machine guns. Additional fuel tanks placed behind the crew compartment added 518 gallons to the fuel load, giving the XP-61E a total of 1,158 gallons of fuel internal. Augmented by four underwing 310 gallon drop tanks, the XP-61E could carry 2,398 gallons — more than enough for an escort mission to Moscow.

The two XP-61E prototypes differed in the canopy and weapons arrangement: the first prototype had the canopy hinged on the port side, lifting upward, with the four nose guns mounted in pairs above and below each other. The second prototype had a rear sliding canopy and had the guns mounted in line straight across the nose. Although the performance of the XP-61E easily surpassed any production P-61, it could not match the performance of the North American F-82 Twin Mustang which won the Long Range Escort Fighter contract.

XP-61F, P-61G and P-61H

There were three variants of the P-61 that were never put into service, in fact, two were never actually built. The XP-61F designation was used for a P-61C (43-8338) that was to be modified by Northrop as a two seat night-fighter. The aircraft was accepted and delivered to the Army on 10 August 1945, then bailed back to Northrop for the necessary modifications to the XP-61F configuration and testing. There is no record as to whether or not the aircraft was ever actually modified or what those modifications consisted of. During October of 1945 the aircraft was sent to a storage facility.

The P-61G actually flew; however, the designation P-61G was never officially assigned by the Army. Sixteen P-61B-20s were modified at the Douglas Aircraft Company's Tulsa, Oklahoma, plant for the weather reconnaissance mission. The SCR-720 Airborne Intercept (AI) radar was replaced by a General Electric APS-10 weather radar, the dorsal turret was removed, some additional radios were added and air sampling instrumentation was installed. Sixteen aircraft were completed, but only fourteen were operational with the 4185th AAF Base Unit at Independence, Kansas. During 1946 these aircraft were sent to other Air Material Command bases to be used in weather research projects like THUNDERSTORM, or to operational Air Defense Command units for use as hack aircraft.

The P-61H was a proposal to replace the dorsal turret with a large fuel tank which would project above the fuselage. Although never put into production, the installation of a ferry tank was not a new idea. Many Pacific-based P-61s had the fuselage ferry tank of a B-24 fitted in place of the dorsal turret for the long flight across the Pacific. This modification was done to both P-61As and P-61Bs. The tanks were promptly removed after the aircraft landed at their permanent base of operations and replaced with the four gun dorsal turret.

The XP-61E was originally designed as a long range escort fighter to cover SAC missions deep into Russia. The center fuselage pod was completely redesigned for the day-fighter mission with the armament in the nose and a tandem cockpit with a bubble canopy. (Northrop)

The second XP-61E prototype differed from the first in that the four .50 caliber machine guns were arranged horizontally rather than in the vertical box arrangement used on the first aircraft. The second aircraft also had a sliding canopy, while the first prototype had a canopy that was hinged to open to the left. (AFM)

Fuselage Development

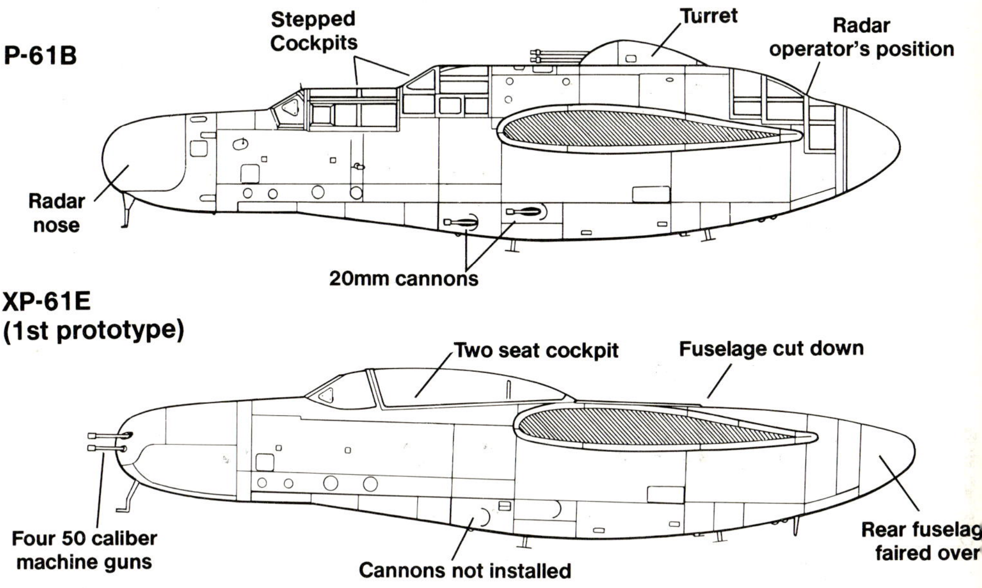

The first flight of the XP-61E prototype took place during January of 1945. There were two XP-61Es built, both aircraft being modified from P-61B-10 airframes, retaining the booms and wings. (Northrop)

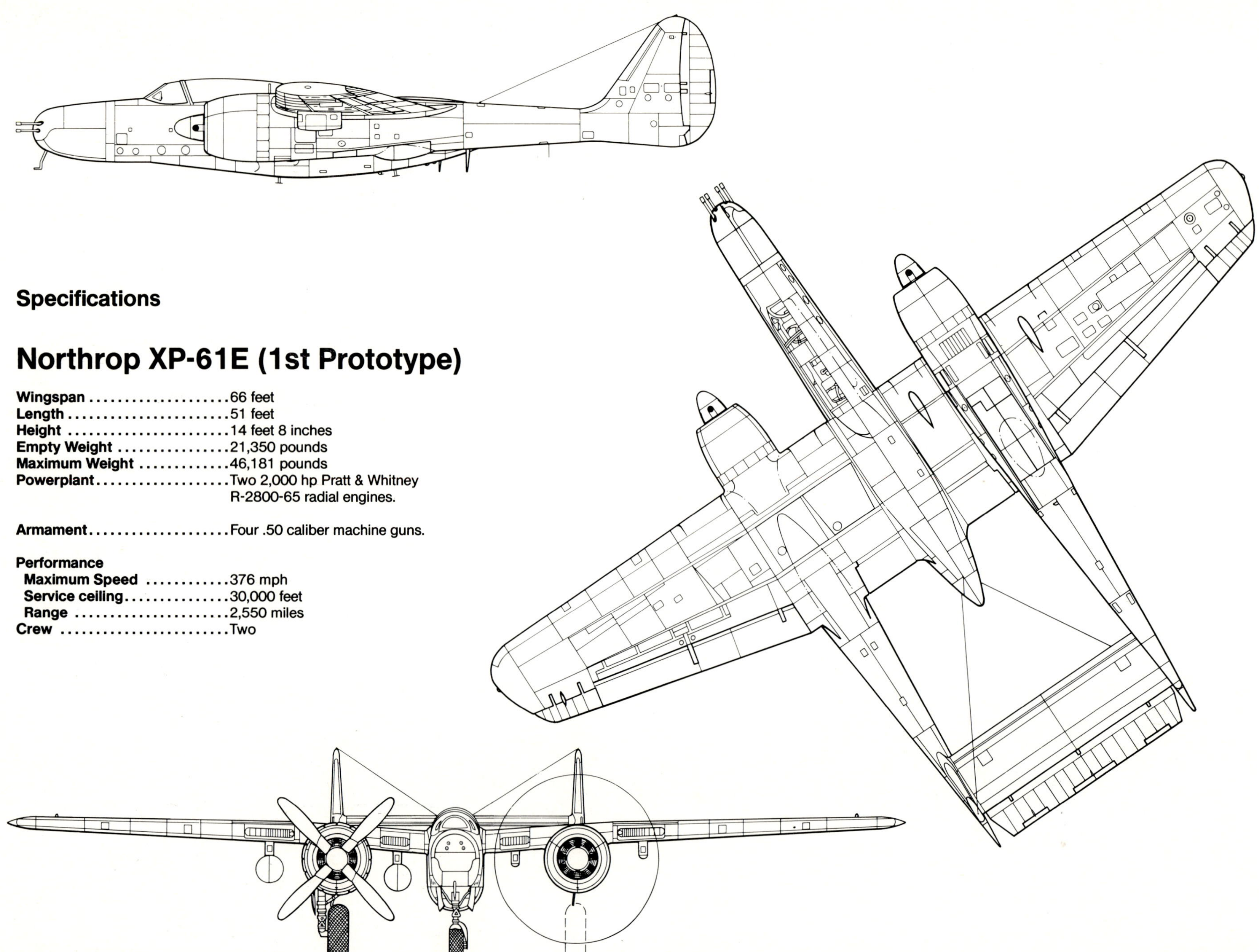

Specifications

Northrop XP-61E (1st Prototype)

Wingspan .... 66 feet
Length .... 51 feet
Height .... 14 feet 8 inches
Empty Weight .... 21,350 pounds
Maximum Weight .... 46,181 pounds
Powerplant .... Two 2,000 hp Pratt & Whitney R-2800-65 radial engines.

Armament .... Four .50 caliber machine guns.

Performance
Maximum Speed .... 376 mph
Service ceiling .... 30,000 feet
Range .... 2,550 miles
Crew .... Two

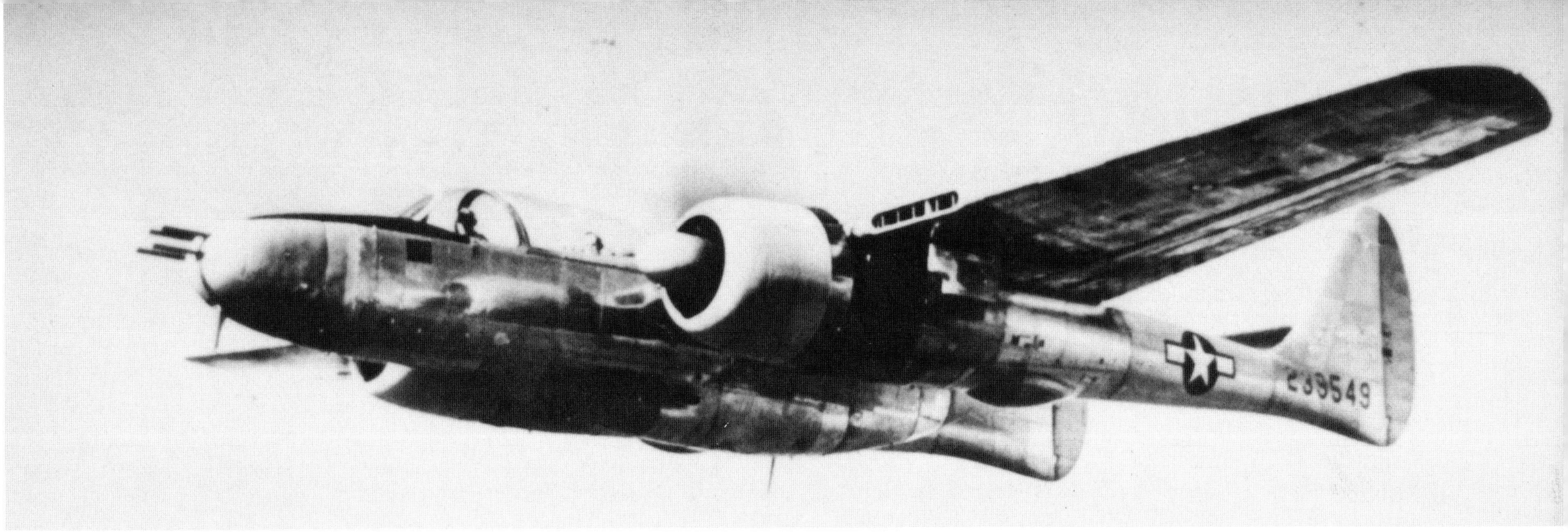

The first XP-61E prototype on a test flight over California. The aircraft had Yellow cowlings and spinners, common markings for Northrop prototypes. (Northrop)

XP-61E

1st Prototype

2nd Prototype

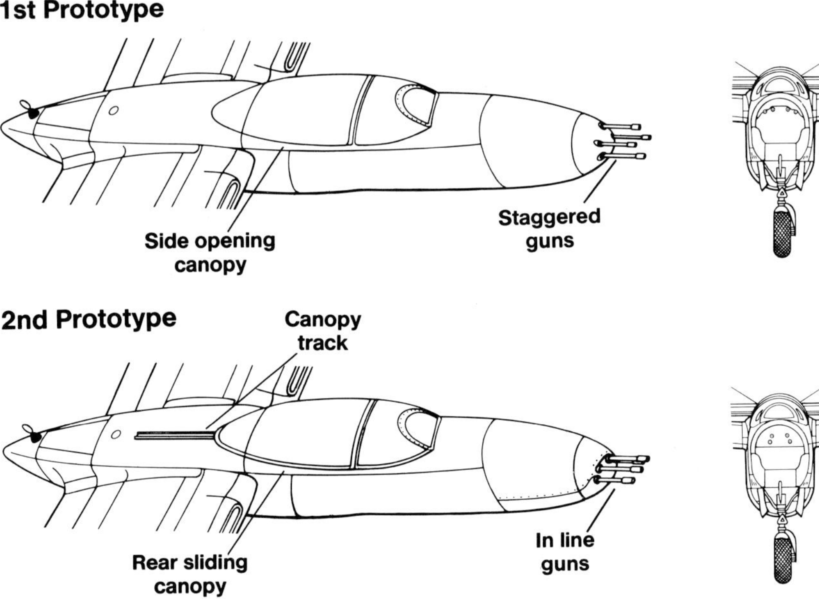

The first prototype on the ramp at Hawthorne. The four .50 caliber machine guns were arranged above and below each other, with the bottom two guns slightly further apart than the top guns. (Northrup)

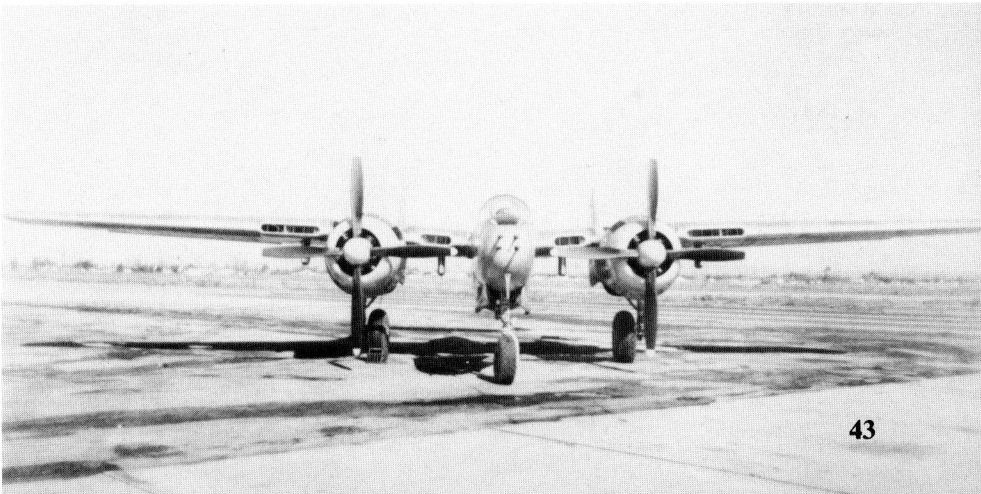

F-15A Reporter

The basic XP-61E design, although it did not meet the Long Range Escort Fighter requirements, did fit another Army requirement — that of a very long range, high altitude, high speed reconnaissance aircraft. Six months after its first flight in the escort fighter configuration, the first XP-61E airframe was returned to Northrop for modification into a reconnaissance aircraft.

The nose guns were replaced by a battery of cameras, the gun ports were faired over and camera ports cut into the sides of the former gun bay. Projected performance figures (based on XP-61E tests) led the Army, in June of 1945, to place a production contract for 175 aircraft under the designation F-15 Reporter and on 3 July 1945, "Slim" Parrett, Northrop's Chief Test Pilot, lifted the XF-15 off on its first flight.

The production F-15A combined features of the XF-15, XP-61 and a standard P-61C airframe. A late production P-61C-1 (43-8335) was modified with the fuselage of the XF-15 and the sliding canopy of the second XP-61E. Powered by the 2,800 hp Pratt & Whitney R-2800C turbo-supercharged engine, the XF-15A first took flight on 17 October 1945.

The F-15A-1 Reporter was identical to the XF-15A except that the P-61C "fighter brakes" were deleted and the camera bay was slightly reconfigured by the Hughes Tool Company. The first production F-15A-1 was accepted by the Army in September of 1946; however, its production was to be short lived. The reasons why the F-15A Reporter was cancelled are unclear, but the primary reason is believed to be that the Air Force knew that high performance piston-engine aircraft like the F-15A were obsolete with jets entering the inventory. During 1947, after thirty-six aircraft were completed, the Army cancelled the remaining 139 aircraft on the production order.

Of the thirty-six aircraft built, nine went to Air Material Command for various research programs. The remaining twenty-seven were issued to the 8th Photo Reconnaissance Squadron based at Johnson Air Base, Japan. The first aircraft arrived by ship during March of 1947. Salt water corrosion had caused so much damage that three of the first four aircraft to arrive had to be scrapped. In June the first pair of flyable F-15As arrived and they flew their first operational mission during July. By October, the 8th PRS was up to full squadron strength — sixteen aircraft.

During 1948, the now separate U.S. Air Force changed the designation of all reconnaissance aircraft from F to RF. Under the new system the F-15As were redesignated as RF-61Cs. On 1 April 1949, after only twenty-two months in service, the RF-61Cs of the 8th PRS were phased out and reassigned to the 35th Maintenance Squadron at Johnson for final disposition and scrapped.

The camera bay of the XF-15/F-15A was hinged to open forward for access to the cameras. The Hughes Tool Company was the subcontractor responsible for the design of the camera nose and its systems. (AFM)

The first XP-61E prototype was modified to the XF-15 long range reconnaissance configuration during June of 1945. The guns were removed and the nose redesigned to accept high resolution aerial cameras. The XF-15 made its first flight on 3 July 1945. (David Menard)

Nine F-15As went to Air Material Command for assignment to research programs such as Project THUNDERSTORM. The F-15s carried markings identical to the THUNDERSTORM P-61s. The Reporter's designation was changed from F-15A to RF-61C during 1948. (via David Menard)

F-15 Development

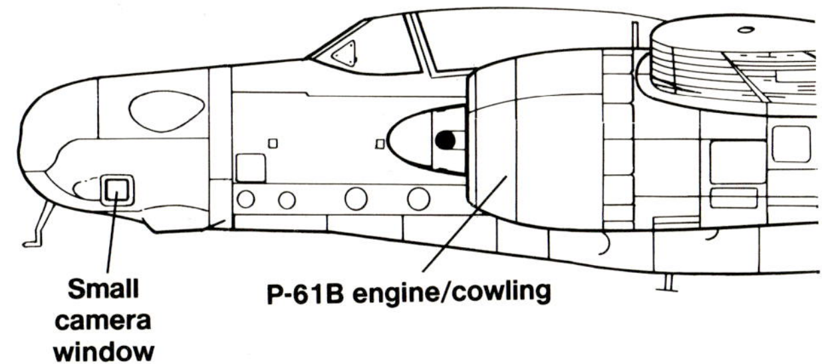

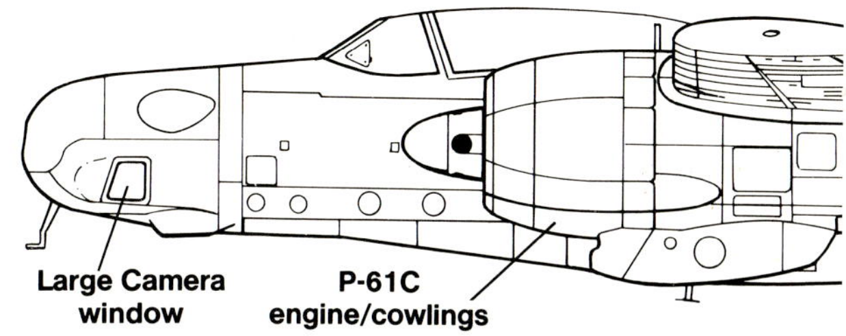

The F-15A-1 production aircraft was externally identical to the second XF-15 test aircraft, with the exception of P-61C engines, a slightly modified camera nose and a sliding canopy. (AFM)

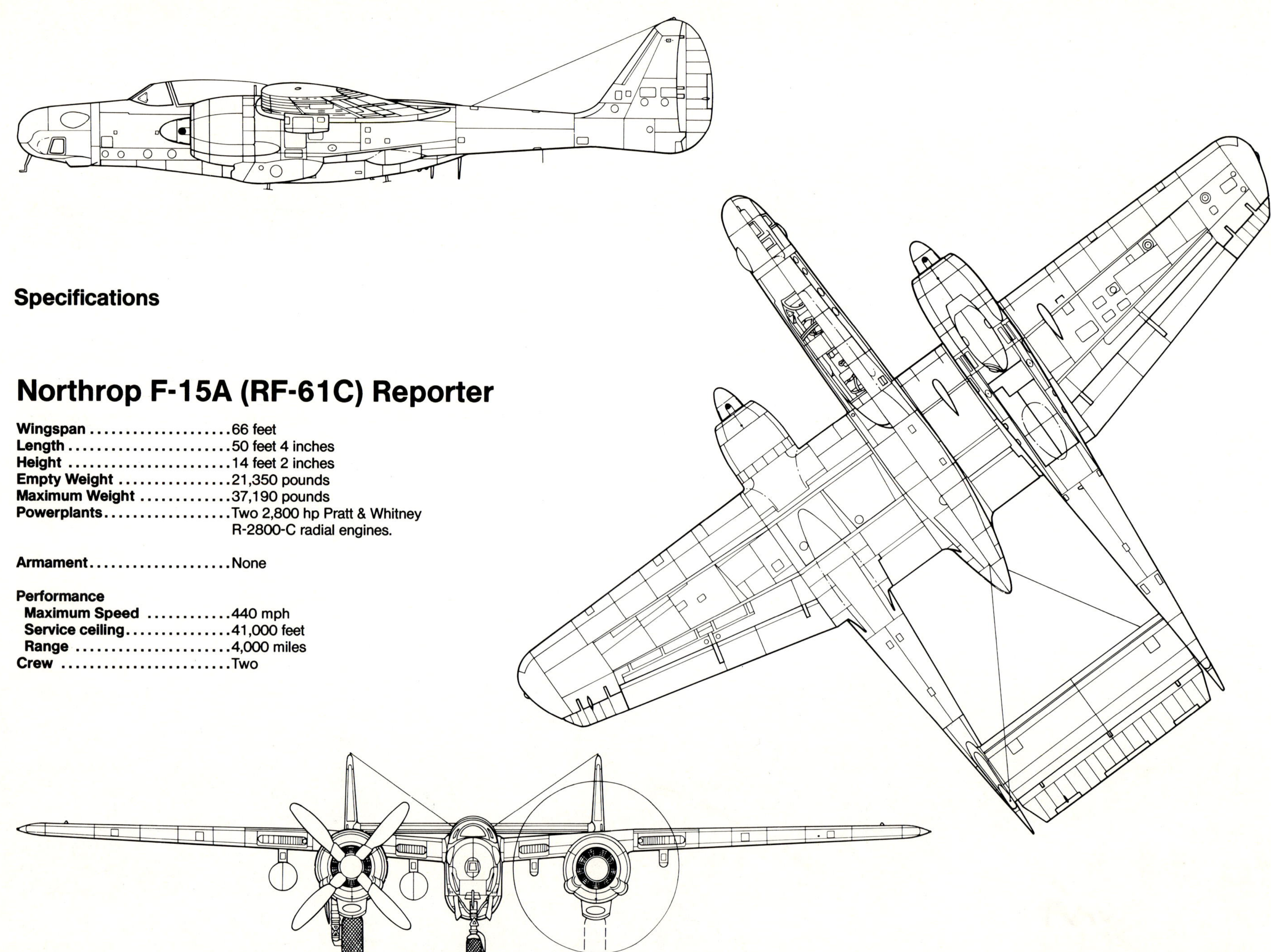

Specifications

Northrop F-15A (RF-61C) Reporter

Wingspan .... 66 feet
Length .... 50 feet 4 inches
Height .... 14 feet 2 inches
Empty Weight .... 21,350 pounds
Maximum Weight .... 37,190 pounds
Powerplants .... Two 2,800 hp Pratt & Whitney R-2800-C radial engines.

Armament .... None

Performance
Maximum Speed .... 440 mph
Service ceiling .... 41,000 feet
Range .... 4,000 miles
Crew .... Two

Although Army Air Force had contracted for 175 F-15A Reporters, only thirty-six were built before the contract was cancelled during 1947. Production F-15As, like this aircraft of the 8th PRS, shared major components with the P-61C except for the different fuselage and the deletion of the fighter brakes. (AFM)

This F-15A of the 8th Photo Reconnaissance Squadron carries a Black eight ball on the fin. The anti-glare panel on the nose was in Olive Drab and all numbers were in Black.

THE MISSING LINK **was an F-15A assigned to the 8th Photo Reconnaissance Squadron at Johnson Air Base, Japan, during 1948. All F-15A reporters were delivered in overall natural metal finish. The 8th PRS F-15s carried a small Red, White, and Blue stripe on the fin tip. (Linkiewicz via David Menard)**

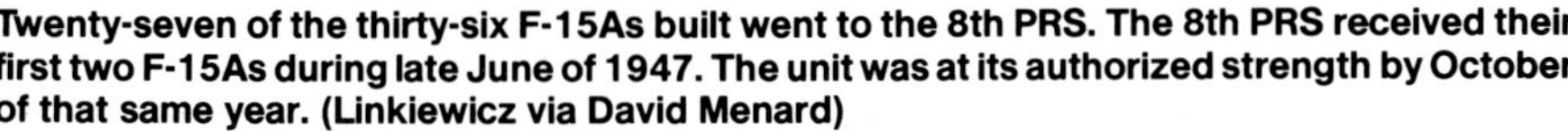

Twenty-seven of the thirty-six F-15As built went to the 8th PRS. The 8th PRS received their first two F-15As during late June of 1947. The unit was at its authorized strength by October of that same year. (Linkiewicz via David Menard)

An F-15A Reporter of the 8th PRS takes off from its home base of Johnson Air Base, Japan. The dark hole in the center of the nose is the camera window for the forward looking oblique camera. (Linkiewicz via David Menard)

The first production F-15A (45-59300) served with the National Advisory Committee for Aeronautics (NACA) before finally being converted to a Borate Bomber with Cal-Nat Airways during 1964. The F-15A crashed on 6 September 1968 near Hollister, California. (Jim Sullivan)

P-61 Nose Art Gallery

BAT OUTA HELL **was a P-61B flown by CAPT Bill Dames of the 548th NFS. (via Warren Thompson)**

SLEEPYTIME Gal **a P-61B of the 421st NFS at Tacloben Island. (via Dave McLaren)**

The *'VIRGIN' WIDOW,* a P-61A of the 6th NFS on Saipan. (Ernest Thomas)

MIDNIGHT MENACE **was a P-61A of the 425th NFS (USAF)**

MIDNIGHT MADONNA **was a P-61B of the 549th NFS on Iwo Jima. (via Dave McLaren)**

ANONYMOUS III **Victory Model was flown by Mel Bode of the 548th NFS. (via Dave McLaren)**

CAPT Ernest Thomas, with his radar operator LT John Acre flew *SLEEPY TIME GAL.* (Ernest Thomas)

Blyshaurica II **was a P-61B that was later used for aerial surv work. (Arthur Harrison)**

Dame de la Nuit **(Lady of the Night) was a P-61B of the 421st NFS. (via Dave McLaren)**

USAAF FIGHTERS
IN ACTION

1026

1043

1045

1067

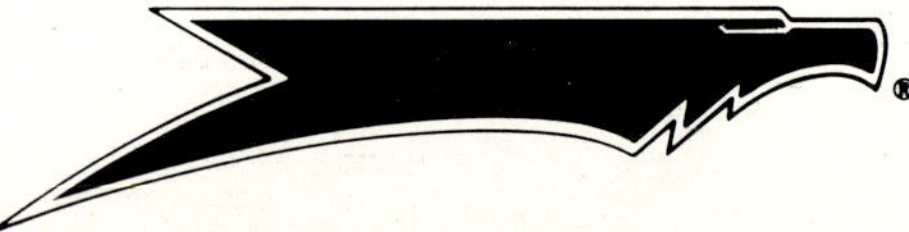

squadron/signal publications